MW00856911

Toll Road Traffic & Revenue Forecasts

An Interpreter's Guide

Toll Road Traffic & Revenue Forecasts

An Interpreter's Guide

Robert Bain

Cover photo credit: © Robert Bain 2009
Cover design by Greg Banks @ BDDesign LLC
This book is printed on acid-free paper.

First edition 2009
Copyright © 2009, Robert Bain
All rights reserved

The right of Robert Bain to be identified as the author of this work has been asserted in accordance with the Copyright, Designs and Patents Act 1988.

No part of this publication may be reproduced or transmitted in any form or by any means, electronic or mechanical, including photocopy, recording, or any information storage and retrieval system, without permission in writing from the author. Permissions may be sought directly from Robert Bain – email: info@robbain.com.

Notice
No responsibility is assumed by the publisher for any injury and/or damage to persons or property as a matter of products liability, negligence or otherwise, or from any use or operation of any methods, products, instructions or ideas contained in the material herein.

British Library Cataloguing in Publication Data
A catalogue record for this book is available from the British Library

ISBN: 978-0-9561527-1-8

Formatting and layout by Angel Editing, Barcelona
Printed and bound by Publicaciones Digitales SA, Seville

10 9 8 7 6 5 4 3 2

PREFACE

I have been working with traffic forecasting models for over twenty years; initially as a transport consultant commissioned to build models, then as a credit analyst evaluating the outputs from models (the traffic and revenue forecasts) and, more recently, as an independent technical reviewer of these models and their forecasts on behalf of investors. After twenty years my principal conclusion is simple. In a world characterised by uncertainty, it is almost certain that traffic forecasts will be wrong.

Step back and consider the modelling accuracy proposition. Could it really be possible to forecast the trip-making patterns of individuals in, say, 2025 with precision – the model's parameters completely and accurately reflecting driver preferences and behaviour, and all of the underlying assumptions and expectations having crystallised as anticipated? No. This usefully moves the discussion forward from stale arguments of assertion about modelling accuracy to a more constructive dialogue about modelling error – its nature and extent – and the important applied consideration of modelling error-tolerance.

An individual's tolerance for modelling error will be dictated by the purpose for which traffic forecasts are made. If we are designing a new road and have to decide whether it should have two lanes or four, we may be able to accommodate a relatively wide range of modelling error. If, on the other hand, we are assessing whether or not an aggressively-structured and finely-sculpted financing schedule for a new toll road will ensure that debt servicing obligations will be met in full and on time, all other things being equal our tolerance is considerably reduced. Traffic and revenue forecasts can only be evaluated within the context for which they are being used – and in credit analysis, that means setting them against other sources of project risk and examining them within the contractual and funding structure specific to a particular deal.

In financial services generally, our modelling error tolerance tends to be low. Toll road scheme sponsors and their financial engineers typically place greater reliance on predictive accuracy (and revenue dependability) than the empirical evidence – reviewed in this guide – would support. For the credit analyst, this brings sensitivity analysis centre-stage. However for sensitivity analysis to be of most help, we need to ensure that the sensitivities are crafted around a base case that represents reasonable assumptions about the future. Base cases designed to tell a specific story or sell a particular deal to market participants are less useful and the results from any sensitivity testing will, at best, remain confusing.

This guide aims to arm the users of traffic forecasts with an understanding of the modelling process and introduces some simple tools that can help to interpret these forecasts. Much of it is based on level-headed, reasonable judgement. We can attach more credibility to a simple traffic story that immediately accords with intuition ('feels right') than a complicated story that requires considerable, detailed and complex explanations in support. There is no substitute for common sense. I hope that you find the guide useful.

Robert Bain
www.robbain.com

Acknowledgements

The author would like to thank the European Investment Bank (EIB) for commissioning an earlier version of this guide for internal publication. The guide has subsequently been extended and expanded yet the author remains grateful to EIB staff for their original help, guidance and contributions. The views expressed here, however, are the author's own and do not necessarily reflect the position of the EIB. The author retains sole responsibility for any errors that remain in this extended version of the guide.

CONTENTS

1. Introduction

This Guide

Purpose of the Guide

This guide has been prepared for the users of traffic and revenue forecasts; primarily those involved in the credit analysis of tolled highway facilities (roads, bridges and tunnels). It is not designed to teach the principles of traffic modelling – although a number of these principles are summarised in the following pages. Rather, it has been developed to aid interpretation and to promote informed debate and discussion about the inputs into and outputs from traffic forecasting models.

Traffic and revenue study reports come in many guises. To the reader whose expertise lies elsewhere, they are often daunting documents containing specialist language and technical detail, incorporating sophisticated mathematics, and running to hundreds of pages. These characteristics should not disguise the fact that traffic models remain crude and incomplete simplifications of what are, in real life, complex and evolving patterns of individual decision-making about travel and interactions with transport supply networks. The outputs from forecasting models should always be viewed cautiously and in the context of their inherent limitations.

Nevertheless, when applied appropriately traffic models provide useful insights into road users' likely behavioural responses to possible future states of the world. They facilitate the testing of alternative transport and travel propositions, and the examination of the sensitivity of outputs (traffic volumes by link) to changes in key input variables.

Reading the pages that follow will not turn you into a traffic modeller (so don't worry!). It will, however, shine a light on some of the issues that traffic advisers have to address, some of the techniques at their disposal and some of the practical constraints that they face.

Familiarity with the process – albeit from a high-level – holds the potential to improve the interface between those who have to interpret and use toll road traffic and revenue forecasts and those who prepare them. Many traffic advisers develop a keen insight into the issues they are trying to model on specific projects; sometimes beyond their model's capabilities. Tap into that insight and you will get more from your traffic adviser.

Scope of the Guide

The primary focus of this guide is revenue forecasting; how people do it, what to look for and what can go wrong – unintentionally (error) or intentionally (bias). The target reader is the credit analyst and the assets under the spotlight are drawn from the toll road sector. The guide should also be of interest to the broader constituency of project counterparties interested in infrastructure investment and, in particular, future cash flow dependability – and it retains a relevance beyond toll roads. Switch from road to rail for a minute and consider one of the greatest feats of 20th century engineering in Europe; the Channel Tunnel.

> *"What was not known at the time was that the railways' predictions of passenger demand...were a sham. A senior official...admitted last year that the forecasts were deliberately optimistic in order to make the business case for the tunnel. The original forecast was for the trains to carry 17m passengers in 2003; in the event, the figure was a little over 7m. If accurate forecasts had been made at the time, the tunnel would never have been built."*
>
> The Guardian, 7th April 2004

In high profile, big ticket transactions when lending is based on single-asset, demand-driven cash flows alone – not balance sheet strength – infrastructure investment becomes a high stakes game with powerful incentives at play. The forecasting process, imperfect from the start, is seldom insulated from these incentives. Credit analysts need to be asking the right questions of their technical advisers and having an understanding of the forecasting process is an important prerequisite in that regard. This is as true for toll roads as it is for other transportation projects (and in other sectors) when limited-recourse lenders are exposed to market risk.

Structure of the Guide

The remainder of this chapter sets the scene by placing traffic risk in the broader context of the project risks which can impact on tolled highway scheme cash flows. Traffic risk is not homogenous, however, so some examination of its potential characteristics (and the role of various mitigants) is provided. At the end of Chapter 1, the attention turns to credit analysis and the impact that traffic risk plays in terms of the overall assessment of a project's credit quality and vulnerabilities.

Chapter 2 introduces traffic forecasting and outlines the various stages involved in the construction of a typical transport model. The ways in which the demand and supply characteristics of local travel markets are represented are described – as are the types of survey at the modeller's disposal. Traffic forecasting is examined, particularly in the context of how growth is treated, and the relationship between traffic and revenue forecasts is explained. The chapter closes with a review of key model inputs and a summary of the transport modelling process in its entirety.

Chapter 3 turns the spotlight on traffic forecasting risk. An evidence-based approach is used in the form of a literature review. This is followed by consideration of some of the more common sources of modelling error – and, hence, predictive failure. The chapter concludes with a description of how uncertainty can be incorporated within the forecasting process itself.

Finally, Chapter 4 steps back from the detail of transport modelling and the review of predictive accuracy to suggest alternative approaches that can be taken to the analysis of traffic forecasts. This is followed by observations about best practice in terms of the format and content of traffic and revenue forecasting reports; responding to the fact that – in some cases – there appears to be limited appreciation of where investor scrutiny will be focussed. Ways in which forecasts can be inflated are described, so that analysts can watch out for such tricks, and a summary checklist is presented at the end of the chapter – prompting analysts to review their understanding of the key issues relevant to any toll road traffic and revenue study.

A glossary and four appendices complement this guide. The glossary focuses on technical terms commonly found in toll road traffic study reports. Appendix A contains a comprehensive checklist for assessing a toll road project's possible exposure to forecasting risk; the Traffic Risk Index template developed by Standard & Poor's. Two worked examples of the Traffic Risk Index – illustrating alternative approaches – are presented in Appendices B and C. Appendix D outlines a recommended table of contents for traffic and revenue studies aimed specifically at an investor audience.

TOLL ROAD PROJECT RISKS – OVERVIEW

Project Risks and Their Allocation

Toll road concessions share many of the risk characteristics associated with other privately-financed infrastructure projects. Pre-construction risks include securing site plans, permits and licences, environmental-related risks (such as gaining EIS[1] approval), and risks associated with facility design. Construction risks themselves are commonly a (if not the) major risk associated with any new-build project. Immediate post-construction risks include testing and commissioning risk; prior to project operations.

In the operational phase of toll road projects, risks include those arising from competing routes and possibly competing modes, tolling systems/technologies and – of course – traffic volume risk. In addition there are risks associated with operations and maintenance responsibilities, and with the requirement to hand-back the asset to the public sector at the end of the concession term. Aside from these there are the usual political, legal, regulatory, economic, force majeure and financing risks which impact on every privately-financed infrastructure project to a greater or lesser extent. A typical high-level risk allocation matrix is presented in Table 1.1.

---

[1] Environmental Impact Statement.

TABLE 1.1: TOLL ROAD CONCESSION RISK ALLOCATION MATRIX[2]

Risk Category	Risk Allocation	
	Public Sector	Private Sector
Project Delivery Risks		
Planning/Permitting Issues	✓	
Environmental Issues	✓	
Site/Ground Conditions		✓
Archaeology & Fossils	✓	
Protesters		✓
Latent Defects		✓
Design		✓
Construction		✓
Commissioning		✓
Revenue Risks		
Traffic Volume		✓
Tolling System		✓
Competing Routes	✓	✓
Change in Law Risk	✓	✓
Force Majeure Risk		✓
Operations & Maintenance Risks		
Maintenance & Lifecycle		✓
Technological Obsolescence		✓
Asset Handback		✓
Financial Risks		
Funding Availability	✓	
Financing Risk		✓
Refinancing Gain	✓	✓
Interest/Exchange Rates		✓

---

[2] This risk matrix is provided for illustration only. Some risks may be shared between the public and private sectors. Risk allocation varies and has to be understood on a project-by-project basis.

In most toll road concessions the majority of project risks are transferred to the private sector. In the UK, the public sector retains so few risks on its road concessions that it identifies in contracts only its retained risks. All other risks are assumed to be the private sector's responsibility. The UK Highways Agency's retained risks are:

- Land acquisition,
- Change orders (instigated by the Highways Agency),
- Unforeseeable archaeology,
- Compensation for the concessionaire, should the Highways Agency impose user-paid tolls on its shadow toll roads (described later).

Looking over risk allocation matrices across a range of projects it quickly becomes apparent that the key distinguishing feature of most toll road projects – compared with other infrastructure-based public private partnerships – is that they expose financiers to demand (traffic) risk[3].

Traffic Risk

Before examining traffic risk in any shape, let us be quite clear that, from a credit perspective, it is lender exposure to revenue risk that is the central focus; not traffic risk per se. The two risks may be linked – and commonly are – yet there are an increasing number of performance and availability-based road projects being developed globally wherein payments are made to private-sector concessionaires irrespective of asset usage. That is not to say that analysts reviewing such projects should have no interest in traffic forecasts. Predictions of future traffic volumes – particularly for heavy vehicles – are used for maintenance expenditure profiling, for example. However the analytical starting point with any tolled facility is the key question:

To what extent are lenders exposed to demand revenue risk?

---

[3] Other transport projects may expose lenders to demand risk (such as trams). Much of the advice contained in this guide is equally applicable under such circumstances.

Toll road projects come in an increasing number of varieties. At one end of the spectrum is the availability-based construct mentioned above (in which case analysts can move fairly quickly through most traffic issues). At the other end of the spectrum is the conventional toll road with full, unfettered lender exposure to traffic – and hence revenue – risk. In between lies a variety of models designed to mitigate/share traffic risk: user-paid toll road projects with minimum traffic or revenue guarantees, with financial re-balancing ('re-equilibrium') mechanisms[4], with return-dependent concession tenors and shadow toll road projects. Minimum revenue guarantees are often sized to cover senior debt in full or a substantial part thereof – in which case analysis should focus on the guarantee itself (and the guarantor), on the gap between the guarantee and the debt servicing obligations, and on the role of toll revenues in terms of plugging that gap.

Under a shadow tolling arrangement the concessionaire is reimbursed based on traffic usage – however payments are made by the public sector procuring agency, not by road users[5]. There is no point-of-use charge imposed and therefore no requirement to calculate 'willingness to pay' (discussed later). Drivers use the facility like any other road; often oblivious to the fact that it is provided and financed by the private sector. The fact that payments are based on traffic use, however, means that – in common with regular user-paid toll roads – lenders are exposed to demand risk. Hence traffic forecasting and the interpretation of traffic forecasts remain important analytical considerations.

Under a shadow tolling arrangement analysts also have to consider the tariff schedule. It may mimic the type of toll structure employed on user-paid toll roads (differentiating by vehicle type) however a number of shadow toll roads – in Spain, Portugal and the UK, for example – additionally incorporate a system of traffic payment 'bands' as outlined in Table 1.2.

---

[4] Such mechanisms re-establish the economic 'balance' of a project if, for example, the project IRR drops below a predetermined threshold.
[5] In some countries shadow tolls are not popular. Lenders would rather have the driving public as their payment counterparty than a government department!

TABLE 1.2: UK SHADOW TOLL PAYMENT BANDS[6]

Traffic Band	Band Size (million vehicle kilometres/year)	Shadow Toll (per vehicle kilometre)
Band One	0 – 70	9p
Band Two	71 – 100	6p
Band Three	101 – 130	3p
Band Four	over 130	0p

The shadow toll payment bands described above have the effect of sharing traffic revenue risk between the public and the private sectors. In most cases, the band definitions are specified by bidders. Band One is commonly used to cover senior debt service and fixed operating & maintenance (O&M) costs. It attracts the highest payment per vehicle kilometre/mile and may be linked to existing traffic volumes (thus enabling senior debt to be retired even under a conservative no-growth scenario). Subsequent bands attract rates lower than Band One. Band Two is often sized to cover variable O&M costs and any sub-debt. Band Three may be used to distribute cash to equity through dividends and for quasi-equity (sponsor loan) debt service. Any traffic in Band Four earns no additional revenue for the concessionaire, capping the obligations of the procuring agency and the concessionaire's returns.

The shadow toll banded payment mechanism outlined above underscores the importance of understanding, not simply traffic risk, but the critical link between toll road traffic and revenue – such that lender's exposure to revenue risk can be assessed. The link between traffic and revenue is revisited later in the context of user-paid toll roads; the dominant model for privately-financed highway facilities worldwide and the focus for the remainder of this guide.

---

[6] The illustrated example shows shadow toll payment bands that reduce as road usage increases. The concessionaire receives most of its payment based upon the lower levels of traffic (about which there is most certainty). In this way, some of the revenue risk is shared with the procuring agency. Although rare, there are some shadow toll road payment mechanisms that work in reverse, rewarding the concessionaire most for higher volumes of traffic. This exacerbates the revenue risk faced by lenders.

Credit Risk Analysis

Before diving deep into traffic, tolls and revenues forecasts, it is worth revisiting some credit fundamentals. In terms of assessing credit quality, exposure to revenue risk is clearly important, although it has to be set within a wider context. Thinly-capitalised toll road projects can experience distress for many reasons other than operating performance. Problems stemming from land non-availability, public opposition, contractor or sub-contractor insolvency, the choice of construction technology or materials, expropriation obligations, contractual misinterpretations and late legal challenges have caused problems in the past – and sit outside of financial models; too often the sole focus for risk assessment and mitigation.

Turn to a key metric of financial credit strength – the Debt Service Coverage Ratio[7] (DSCR). Two toll road projects may share the same minimum and average DSCRs but may react quite differently to sensitivity testing; one being highly sensitive to stresses or shocks while the other remains resilient. Assessments of credit quality should reflect this difference. Similarly, two projects with very different DSCRs may be regarded as being equivalent in terms of credit quality because of comparable sensitivity test performance (and/or other counter-balancing transaction characteristics). Sensitivity testing is discussed in more detail later.

Credit metrics such as financial ratios cannot be viewed in isolation. The financial strength of a project – whether derived from user fees or not – has to be assessed within the context of the transaction's structural provisions and contractual protections for lenders. For this reason, and the ones listed earlier, there are few simple rules-of-thumb when it comes to evaluating the credit quality of tolled highways. There is no magical coverage ratio that defines an investment-grade toll road, bridge or tunnel. Credit analysts need to understand traffic and revenue issues on a project-by-project basis, and a general appreciation of traffic modelling – the focus for the next chapter – is a powerful tool in that regard.

---

[7] The DSCR is the ratio of cash from operations to principal and interest obligations. The ratio should exclude any cash balances that a project could draw on to service debt, such as reserve funds.

2. TRAFFIC MODELLING & FORECASTING

INTRODUCTION

Traffic models are sets of mathematical equations designed to reflect how people make decisions about travel. First developed in the 1950s, they have become progressively more sophisticated over the years however, like most models, they remain simplified representations of much more complex systems. Travel decisions are impacted by many influences such as personal characteristics, family circumstances and choices about trip-making (where to travel, for what purpose, when to travel and how to travel). Traffic models attempt to represent these decisions through mathematical relationships constructed around assumptions about human behaviour and informed by data from existing sources or from new surveys.

Traffic models come in many guises. There is no prescribed process nor consensus for determining which type of model should be used in particular circumstances – other than the fact that it should be fit-for-purpose. Models range from simple spreadsheet-based constructs through to those built using specialist, off-the-shelf software packages[8]. In toll road traffic forecasting, the use of spreadsheet-based models tends to be confined to 'sketch planning' models designed to provide a broad-brush evaluation of facilities at an early stage of design and the preparation of short-term forecasts for mature, established facilities with good historical data. Most toll road traffic forecasts prepared for international investor scrutiny result from the application of one of the popular transportation modelling software packages on the market today.

Although they differ in terms of detail and emphasis, most modelling packages are based on a common methodology used for travel forecasting known as the four-stage (or four-step) procedure. A

---

[8] Widely-used software packages include names such as EMME/2, SATURN, CUBE, TransCAD and PTV Vision.

full, technical description of the four-stage procedure – the theoretical underpinning of traditional travel demand models – happily lies beyond the remit of this guide, however its application in toll road traffic forecasting is so widespread that it merits mention here, if only to introduce some of the concepts and language frequently referred to in traffic and revenue study reports. The four stages in terms of simulating travel behaviour are, sequentially:

- Trip generation
- Trip distribution
- Mode choice
- Trip assignment

Trip generation asks the question: how many trips are generated across the study area? A set of equations or trip rates are used to estimate the number of trips ('trip ends') produced by and – separately – attracted to different parts of the study area based on land use and socio-demographic factors such as residential and employment characteristics.

Trip distribution asks the question: where are the trips going? Trip distribution matches-up all of the trip ends (estimated earlier) creating actual trips. It is assumed that most trips produced in a specific area will travel to accessible locations nearby; relatively few will travel great distances to far-off attractions – mimicking some sort of gravitational interaction between areas. Indeed, the gravity model is still the most widely used formulation of trip distribution – and is commonly referred to in traffic reports. The gravity model suggests that, in the case of two towns, travel between them will increase as the population of one or both increases. However the further the two towns are apart (in terms of time, distance and/or cost) the less will be the movement between them. The outputs from the trip distribution stage are trip matrices (or trip tables) – described later.

Mode choice (or modal split) asks the question: what mode of transport do trip-makers use? Commuters, for example, might choose private car, shared car or van pooling, or public transport – based on the availability and relative attractiveness of the alternative options. In a typical toll road study, mode choice will be a minor consideration. There are relatively few circumstances where public transportation acts as a significant competitive threat to tolled highway facilities. For this reason, many toll road demand models ignore transit services entirely. However if there is modal competition (or, importantly, if there may be in the future – such as a new rail or air service competing against a long-distance toll road), mode choice becomes an important consideration.

Trip assignment asks the question: which route is taken for each trip? This is a (if not the) critical step in toll road forecasting. Trip assignment determines route choice; the path that a traveller takes through the computerised roadway system (network) to reach their desired destination. The most desirable path through the network is assumed to be the one that minimises time or distance or cost for the traveller. These 'best paths' take full account of highway characteristics such as link capacities. When running the traffic model, some paths become popular and congestion builds. The resulting slower, congested travel times are fed back-into the earlier trip distribution stage of the simulation model through a series of iterations so that traffic becomes more realistically dispersed across the whole of the modelled highway network. This is known as equilibrium assignment; equilibrium having been achieved when no driver can improve their route choice.

TRAFFIC FORECASTING: THE USERS' PERSPECTIVE

Thankfully, few credit analysts will be exposed to the traditional four-stage transport modelling process in detail. Indeed, many forecasting practitioners have only a vague understanding of the precise workings of their 'black box' modelling software packages. However the key concepts and associated language find expression in toll road traffic and revenue study reports – hence the introduction to this chapter. The following section steps back from the unpinning theory to consider traffic modelling from a users' perspective. In that context it is useful to think of traffic forecasting models as attempts to replicate and represent the travel 'economy' in the area being studied. That economy is comprised of a supply-side and a demand-side – each of which is introduced separately below.

The Supply-Side of the Travel Economy

The supply-side of the travel economy reflects the configuration of the transportation network. In the case of toll roads, this is primarily highway infrastructure (roads with different features and intersections of different types). The traffic model treats the road network as a series of links or pipes; some are high-speed, high-flow (such as multi-lane expressways) whereas others have a narrower bore (such as residential streets) with lower performance characteristics – see Figure 2.1. The use of a pipe analogy is appropriate as some of the workings of network models actually derive from fluid mechanics![9]

FIGURE 2.1: HIGHWAYS CODED AS A SERIES OF LINKS

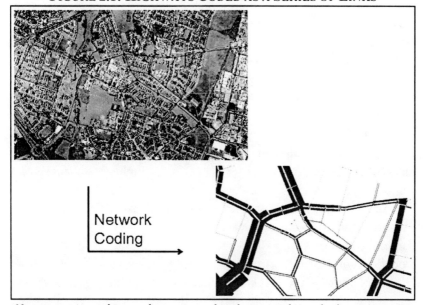

Network
Coding

No attempt is made to code every road in the network – only the major ones.

Intersections may be modelled explicitly – and sometimes in considerable detail (reflecting their geometric design or the amount of green-time that drivers experience on a specific approach to a set of traffic signals). Intersections are often referred to as 'nodes'.

---

[9] Unlike travel behaviour, however, the flow of water in a pipe follows a simple, known equation (flow = inside area * velocity) and therefore can be computed with accuracy.

Alternatively the characteristics of intersections can be represented in less detail. The delay that an intersection imposes on drivers may be reflected in the characteristics ascribed to the links that feed into it, for example.

The modeller's selection of the level of detail to use to describe (code) a highway network will be guided by many factors, not least of which will be the level of detail required from the model outputs. Data and time availability, and the level of resources to hand usually place practical constraints on the level of modelling detail. The language used in traffic and revenue reports typically gives some insight. A 'simulation model' would be expected to lie at the more detailed end of the spectrum, whereas a 'strategic model' suggests the use of a broader-brush approach. Once again, there is no right or wrong method – only tools that are fit for the purpose to hand. Importantly, however, there is no evidence to suggest that greater modelling detail or effort systematically improves predictive accuracy.

In terms of supply-side (network) representations, traffic forecasters may have to construct a number of different networks reflecting future highway developments (major new roads, new intersections etc.). This introduces a potential source of modelling error if, in fact, actual highway enhancements depart from earlier modelling expectations – particularly if these highway enhancements complement or compete with the toll road.

Traffic modelling is frequently described as being part science, part art. Modelling the base year supply-side – the representation of the highway network today – is the science part. It is frequently modelled with, literally, military precision using mapping data from GPS satellites. This level of precision does not extend to the representation of the demand-side of the travel economy, however, which exposes the credit analyst to the art of traffic modelling.

The Demand-Side of the Travel Economy

Traffic models do not attempt to simulate trip-making behaviour for every period during the day or week. Modellers concentrate on busy periods and/or times-of-the-day that reflect important and distinguishing trip-making patterns. The most common modelled time period is a weekday morning (AM) peak period – say from 6am – 9am; or an average hour within that period. This 'time slice' may be complemented by separate models for a weekday PM peak period (perhaps an average hour between 4pm – 7pm) and for the inter-peak period that lies in between. If significant, a weekend period should also be modelled. These choices rest with the traffic forecaster and the decision should be based on the nature of the local travel market under examination. Estimating satisfactory models for inter-peak and weekend periods, however, presents particular challenges to traffic modellers. For this reason alone, most traffic studies somewhat conveniently dismiss the significance of inter-peak and weekend travel and focus on peak period modelling exclusively.

The time periods that are modelled are effectively samples. The fewer periods, the smaller the sample – more reliance needing to be placed on factors to expand the sample dataset to reflect daily or annual travel behaviour. Expansion (annualisation) factors are discussed later in this chapter in the context of the relationship between traffic and revenue forecasts – as revenue forecasts are usually required on an annual basis. At the very least, traffic modellers should justify their selection and definition of the time periods being modelled in relation to the characteristics of the toll facility and the local travel market under examination.

Traffic models do not attempt to represent individuals' trip-making behaviour — instead they reflect aggregate trip-making. The area under study is divided into zones[10] generally characterised by having homogenous land use characteristics (eg. a residential district) or containing a major traffic attraction such as a shopping mall. Zones are where trips in the model begin and end. They are small in and around that part of the study area of most interest to the modeller; allowing for detailed analysis. They get progressively larger away from the focus of the study where less detail is required.

Land use and socio-demographic information is collected for each zone such as the current and expected levels of population, households, commercial floorspace, car ownership and employment. To facilitate this, a traffic model's zone boundaries will often be defined to provide a degree of compatibility with census areas. Depending upon the application, the data may be used in the model for different purposes such as the derivation of base or future-year trip

---

[10] Known as 'travel analysis zones' (TAZs) in the United States.

generation estimates. The important issue is that the spatial unit of analysis in forecasting models is the traffic zone. These are numbered and this allows travel behaviour – whether estimated from synthetic generation/distribution models or revealed from survey observations – to be described in terms of demand matrices (known also as 'trip tables'). A demand matrix for a simple three zone traffic model is presented in Figure 2.2:

FIGURE 2.2: ILLUSTRATIVE DEMAND MATRIX

		To Zone...			
		1	2	3	Total
From Zone...	1	0	13	35	48
	2	4	0	0	4
	3	23	1	0	24
	Total	27	14	35	76

The data in Figure 2.2 is interpreted as follows:

- 13 trips are made from Zone 1 to Zone 2
- 23 trips are made from Zone 3 to Zone 1
- No trips are made from Zone 2 to Zone 3
- A total of 24 trips are generated by Zone 3 (the row total)
- A total of 14 trips are attracted to Zone 2 (the column total)
- The total number of trips recorded is 76 (the matrix total)

Note that the leading diagonal in the demand matrix is populated by zeros. This is common in traffic models where short, inter-zonal movements (eg. from Zone 1 to Zone 1) are not accounted for. In toll road studies this tends not to be a significant issue as toll roads are seldom attractive to short-distance trip-makers.

Demand matrices represent the output from the trip distribution stage of the four-stage transport model. They can also be compiled from survey data. At Roadside Interview (RSI) survey stations, for example, a sample of drivers are stopped and asked – amongst other things – where they are travelling to and from. This origin and destination information is then coded (attributed to their respective zones) and the sample data is expanded to represent all drivers passing the survey station (many, if not most, of whom will not have been surveyed). This introduces further potential for sampling error. Moreover, RSIs will only be conducted at selected locations (a) introducing the potential for yet more sampling error, and (b) meaning that some (commonly most) zone-to-zone movements will only be partially observed or will not be observed at all. In Figure 2.2, no trip-making is recorded from Zone 2 to Zone 3. Maybe nobody travelled? Maybe nobody was observed travelling? The analyst does not know.

Other survey techniques can be employed to construct demand matrices. People may be interviewed in their homes (household interviews) or be asked to keep travel diaries. Both techniques – and some others – record trip origin and destination information that later can be coded into their respective zones. Notwithstanding, these survey techniques rely upon sampling, and the sample sizes used in traffic studies tend to be small.

In practice, the construction of the demand matrices used in most toll road studies seldom relies on trip generation/distribution relationships estimated from first principles or from (new) survey data alone. In many parts of the world, some form of traffic model already exists and some demand matrices have already been compiled. It is most common for traffic forecasters to take these existing matrices and build on them; using updated information or providing more level of detail in and around the area of most interest.

Linking Demand & Supply

Transport model zones attach to highway networks via links known as centroid connectors. These connectors enable traffic to join or leave the network from the zones and usually follow the local street pattern (such as the main entrance to a residential neighbourhood).

The process of traffic routeing through a network on the way from one zone to another is called assignment. Specific mathematical rules govern assignment however the general principle is that drivers will use the cheapest route (the minimum cost path) to travel from their origin zone to their destination zone. It is important to note that, in this context, 'cost' refers to a blend of time and money costs. As such, it is termed generalised cost.

Consider the following example:

- Generalised cost (GC) = α(time) + β(toll)
- The value of travel time savings[11] is 8c/minute
- The toll is €1

- The journey time using the toll road is 10 minutes
- The journey time using the free road is 30 minutes

- Therefore the generalised cost of using the free road is:
- $GC_{(free)}$ = (30 * 8c) + €0 = €2.40

- ...and the generalised cost of using the toll road is:
- $GC_{(toll)}$ = (10 * 8c) + €1 = €1.80

As the toll road is cheaper in generalised cost terms, drivers are assumed by the model to use it rather than the free road. The toll road offers time savings and, in the case above, drivers are willing to pay to enjoy these time savings – hence they use the road. This simple concept lies at the heart of most toll road traffic forecasting models.

It has already been noted that traffic assignment is an iterative process which takes explicit account of congestion levels across the network. Speed/flow relationships govern the speeds that result from particular levels of flow (volumes of traffic). As more traffic tries to use a cheap link – the quickest path – speeds deteriorate and journey times increase to a point at which the link ceases to be the cheapest path and traffic starts to use alternative low-cost routes. The iterative process continues until traffic is spread across all of the relevant links. In technical language, the model converges to a steady-state equilibrium.

---

[11] The value of travel time savings is the monetary value assigned to time saved by users of a transportation system. It is a key concept in toll road traffic forecasting.

There are various ways in which a toll road can be represented in a network model. It can be coded as a link with an additional cost reflecting the toll tariff. This 'cost' is translated to a time penalty, and that time penalty is taken into account by the model during its traffic assignment stage – in terms of dictating which travellers use the toll road and which do not. Essentially the link attractiveness is degraded. Trip-makers will use the toll road only if the time savings outweigh the additional cost.

An alternative approach employs the logit model[12] – a simple binary-choice model used for predicting the proportion of traffic which would use a toll road based on its competitive characteristics. By competitive characteristics, we typically mean the cost and time involved travelling on the toll road relative to the cost and time involved travelling on a competing, toll-free facility. Other preferences or biases that impact upon drivers' route choices can also be incorporated into logit models if they are found to impact on route choice – such as a dislike of start/stop traffic conditions or high volumes of trucks.

Traffic forecasters may estimate and use a number of logit models to distinguish among travellers (market segments) with different characteristics or travelling for different reasons (trip purposes). Figure 2.3 shows the characteristic 'S' shaped curve[13] associated with a logit model. In this simplified example, the horizontal axis reflects the difference in travel times between the toll road and a toll-free competitor. Given that difference, the vertical axis indicates the proportion of traffic that would use the toll road.

---

[12] Traffic reports variously refer to logit models as toll diversion models or choice probability curves.

[13] The technical name for this S-shaped curve is the 'choice frontier'.

FIGURE 2.3: ILLUSTRATIVE ROUTE CHOICE LOGIT MODEL

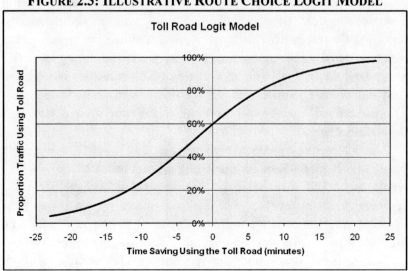

Figure 2.3 shows that when the travel time on the toll road equals that of its toll-free competitor – when the difference between them is zero – the traffic does not split evenly between the two alternatives. The toll road is generally preferred (60%). This may seem counterintuitive in the simplified context of travel time, however it is often suggested in the wider context of generalised costs. It is a characteristic of most traffic forecasting studies and reflects a preference bias, all things being equal, for travel on toll roads. It is commonly referred to as the toll road (or modal) premium and is discussed later in this guide. Logit models are usually estimated from Stated Preference survey data; one of a number of popular survey techniques employed by traffic forecasters – to which this guide now turns.

TRAFFIC & DRIVER SURVEYS

Traffic forecasters have a range of survey techniques at their disposal to provide a snap-shot of local trip-making characteristics and travel patterns. Before defining a survey programme the forecaster will review existing sources of data collected for previous studies or as part of any local rolling programme of surveys. Surveys are expensive to conduct so the forecaster will tend to use them selectively to in-fill for missing or out-of-date information, or to gain more granularity of detail in terms of the toll road being studied. Some of the more commonly applied approaches are summarised below under 'traffic surveys' and 'driver surveys'.

Traffic Surveys

These include:

- **Automatic traffic counts** (ATCs). These use in or on-road detectors to automatically count vehicles (or vehicle axles – which are subsequently converted into vehicle-equivalents). They provide data about traffic (link) volumes by direction, by time of day, by day of week, by month of year etc.
- **Manual traffic counts.** These use surveyors to count vehicles and hence are more costly and less flexible than ATCs. However they provide data that ATCs can not (for example, the number of vehicles making specific turning movements at intersections or the traffic mix classified into motorcycles, cars, buses, trucks etc.).
- **Journey time surveys**. Survey teams record, in their cars, the time it takes to travel from point to point along specific routes (usually routes that compete with the toll road) at particular times of the day or on particular days of the week. This is later compared with modelled journey times and the model is calibrated to reflect observed travel conditions.
- **Roadside interview surveys** (RSIs). Mentioned already, these surveys involve stopping a sample of drivers (or conducting the survey where drivers are stopped anyway eg. at traffic signals) and asking questions about them and their trip-making. Origin and destination information is collected to be later coded into zones and fed-into the construction of the demand matrix(ces). Additional information may be recorded regarding vehicle occupancy, trip-making frequency, the driver's income category etc. A variation on this survey type is the postcard mail-back survey – postcards containing survey questions being handed out to drivers for them to be completed later and mailed back to the survey team.

- **Household interview surveys**. These are alternative methods for collecting trip origin and destination information (and other data) by surveying people in their homes. Travel diaries may be used to build-up a picture of people's trip-making patterns over a period (such as one week).

This list of surveys is not exhaustive. Other survey types include number plate matching surveys, video surveys, interviews with sub-groups of drivers (eg. truckers) etc. Survey programmes should reflect the particular issues being examined by traffic modellers and the nature of their investigations. As stated at the outset, many survey types are expensive to conduct and cost constraints commonly dictate which techniques are used and how they are applied – including, critically, the definition of sample sizes.

Driver Surveys

Two behavioural survey techniques commonly used to support toll road traffic modelling are known as revealed preference and stated preference surveys. Revealed preference simply refers to observing what people do or how they react to choice situations. Standing at a fork in the road counting the number of vehicles using a toll road as opposed to an alternative free road would be an example of a revealed preference survey (although more information would be required for these observations to be of use to forecasters). The point is that the choice that drivers are observed to make reveals their preference.

Revealed preference surveys are very powerful sources of information. The modeller does not have to make assumptions about how people would react in choice situations. They simply observe and learn. But what if the relevant choice situation does not exist? How could a demand modeller learn about local preferences for using a toll road in a region or country with no existing toll roads? How could a demand modeller learn about local preferences for embracing and using electronic tolling technologies when existing toll roads employ manual toll collection techniques? Stated preference (choice) survey techniques are widely used in such circumstances.

In a stated preference survey, people are presented with hypothetical yet realistic choice scenarios and are asked to state their preference. A very simple example is provided in Figure 2.4.

FIGURE 2.4: TYPICAL STATED PREFERENCE TRADE-OFF

	Free Road	Toll Road
Journey Time	45 minutes	30 minutes
Cost (toll tariff)	€0	€0.60

If a person selects the toll road option, they are suggesting that it is worth paying €0.60 to save 15 minutes on their journey. This infers that the person's value of travel time savings – in this context – is 4c/minute (60/15) or more. This is the monetary equivalent that travellers assign to time savings; time savings being a toll road's key product offering. The value (or values) of time savings are used in the trip assignment stage of the modelling process to determine drivers' route choice – including whether or not they use a toll road. Different values of time savings apply to different market segments and to different trip purposes. An upper-income commuter would be expected to have a higher value of time savings than an off-peak recreational traveller. Values of time savings are a critical concept in forecasting and will commonly be estimated from stated preference surveys.

Stated preference surveys may be designed based on feedback from local focus groups. Focus groups are used to identify the features of roads (or specific journeys) that users like/dislike. Some people might not like driving in congestion conditions, for example, or on poorly-maintained roads – and would pay to avoid such conditions. Well designed stated preference surveys allow the forecaster to examine, not only cost versus time saving trade-offs, but the monetary values that people place on other characteristics of toll road usage – this information being used to estimate the types of probability choice (logit) models described earlier.

Some care needs to be taken with the results from stated preference surveys, however. After all, they reveal what people say they would choose, not necessarily what they would choose in reality when they have to back-up their choices with real commitments. And the answers people provide can be conditioned by the context within which (and how) particular questions are asked. Good survey design by experienced practitioners goes some way to reducing these problems. Stated preference survey methods probably obtain their best results when the attributes of a tolled facility can be clearly defined and articulated. It may prove necessary to mask the precise objective of the survey to avoid 'policy bias' – survey respondents indicating preferences in ways designed to affect policy (such as reacting negatively to a proposal to toll a new river crossing in the hope that it will be provided free of charge).

BASE YEAR MODEL CALIBRATION AND VALIDATION

When traffic forecasting models are initially constructed, they seldom replicate base-year traffic conditions accurately. Traffic flows on some links may be higher or lower than observations and modelled journey times can be wrong. The process of model calibration is used to improve accuracy. This can take many forms such as modifying network coding in relation to the roadway configuration, adjusting link speeds or reviewing some of the key input assumptions (summarised later). The base year model is said to be 'validated' when it successfully reproduces base-year traffic conditions against pre-defined performance criteria such as link or screenline[14] volumes lying within +/-15% of actual values, or travel times within +/-10% of those recorded.

A particularly powerful tool which is often used for traffic model calibration is Matrix Estimation. One of the difficulties faced by traffic modellers when attempting to calibrate a model is that the model's performance may be undermined not by simple supply-side errors (network coding) but by significant demand-side deficiencies (blank cells in the demand matrices). These are difficult to fix as the modeller will not know how many trip-makers should really be travelling between all of the zones in the study area – and there may be more than 1,000 zones! It is common for only a small proportion of the cells in a demand matrix to contain any trip information at all. This can cause problems in terms of accurately reflecting background traffic conditions and congestion levels.

---

[14] A screenline is an imaginary line drawn across a number of typically parallel highways representing a travel corridor (often following a physical barrier such as a river) which is used to analyse aggregate flows from one set of zones or 'sector' to another.

Matrix Estimation takes an existing (deficient) matrix – known as the prior matrix – and uses recently observed traffic counts from links across the network to adjust the matrix. The technique uses a powerful statistical method called maximum likelihood estimation to best-fit the matrix to the observed counts. Basically, it comes up with the demand matrix – not certain – but most likely to have created the observed traffic counts, given the available information.

Modelling purists shy from reaching for Matrix Estimation too quickly. Although their matrix may be deficient in some sense(s), it may have been built from many observations gathered over a long period. These are records of trip-making that people actually made and heavy-handed use of Matrix Estimation could transform the matrix from an (albeit deficient) observed matrix to a synthetic matrix; somewhat divorced from reality. The use of Matrix Estimation can also have some undesirable side effects (resulting in trip distribution distortion, for example) so it is right to tread cautiously. It is such a powerful technique that, under certain circumstances, it can make the most inaccurate matrix replicate observed traffic counts. This is clearly dangerous. The traffic counts look correct and for all intents and purposes the model appears to be calibrated – however the underlying demand matrix remains fundamentally flawed. This is not a robust platform from which accurate forecasts can be made but no one will detect that until the future happens.

Matrix Estimation has a legitimate – possibly essential – place in the traffic modeller's toolkit, but the users of forecasts need to be aware that just because a base year model appears to perform well, does not necessarily mean that the underlying demand matrix is accurate. Toll road traffic forecasting reports commonly place great emphasis on the calibrated base year model (and the various activities – such as surveys – that lead up to it). For credit analysts, however, this is not the end of an important process – it's the start of one. A good base year model is the springboard from which the traffic forecasting process can truly begin.

TRAFFIC FORECASTS

Introduction

In most toll road traffic and revenue study reports you will find some text at the end of the model calibration chapter which reads:

> *"Having successfully calibrated the base year model, it now represents a robust platform from which to prepare future-year traffic forecasts."*

It is easy to gloss over such statements or to take comfort from them without actually considering what is being said. This statement infers that a traffic model which recreates the traffic conditions of today (or appears to) is automatically fit-for-purpose in terms of being able to predict the traffic conditions of tomorrow. This only holds for as long as tomorrow looks like today. A well-calibrated base year model is an important input into the forecasting process but, by itself, gives no insight into or guarantee of predictive performance.

Supply-Side Forecasting

Earlier text described how the supply-side representation (the coded highway network) is recast to represent future years. Major highway developments are incorporated in a series of future-year networks. Not every year will be modelled – just key years perhaps coinciding with major developments in the study area coming on-stream. Two possible sources of error are introduced at this stage. The anticipated highway enhancements may not be developed as expected – or the timing associated with them may change. Notwithstanding, future supply-side assumptions tend to be a much smaller source of uncertainty than those associated with future travel demand.

Demand-Side Forecasting

Demand-side forecasting is an art – probably best described as a black art! A multiplicity of approaches can be taken to incorporate growth in traffic models and, it should be emphasised from the outset, the majority of them are relatively unsophisticated.

A simple approach is to apply a single growth factor (say 2% per annum) across the whole of a trip matrix; extrapolating each of the cell values based perhaps on some historical relationship between traffic growth and GDP in the area, and projections of future GDP growth. Use of this simple and crude approach tends to be restricted to circumstances under which the traffic modeller has very limited socio-demographic or land use data – or in host jurisdictions in which such data is unreliable or does not exist.

A marginally more advanced technique is to adjust the demand matrices' row and column totals in line with the growth projected for planning variables such as population or employment levels across the study area. Referring back to Figure 2.2 (page 16), the row total in a demand matrix represents the total number of trips generated by (exiting from) a zone. The column total represents all of the trips attracted to (entering) a zone. Population growth projections are commonly used to guide the future number of trips generated by a residential zone, whereas employment growth projections are used to give insight into the future number of trips attracted to a zone in a city's downtown commercial centre. There are a number of variants on this approach and analysts should refer to specific traffic study reports (and their authors) for deeper insight in this regard. However many toll road forecasters focus on making adjustments to the row and column totals in a demand matrix; these adjustments being based on assumptions about how zonal trip-making may change in response to anticipated demographic or land use developments. In short, a fairly simple and blunt approach is taken to incorporating demand growth in most toll road forecasting models. This is state-of-the-practice (the applied science of traffic modelling has developed little further than this) and represents one of the most significant limitations in terms of any transportation model's predictive dependability.

Having adjusted the row and column totals upwards, the values in each of the cells now fail to add-up to these new row and column totals. An iterative mathematical process called 'furnessing'[15] is used to re-balance the individual cell (zone-to-zone) values to match the new totals. This is way beyond the scope of this guide, but use of this

---

[15] This process may also be referred to in reports as use of the Fratar Algorithm.

common technique places a very important constraint on how well traffic models can adapt to future conditions. This constraint is known as the 'fixed trip matrix constraint' – widely recognised in traffic modelling circles but seldom shared with the outside world.

When any highway improvement takes place (such as the build of or extension to a toll road) several changes in trip-making patterns can result. One is reassignment. Traffic travelling from A to B may transfer to a different route – perhaps to the toll road. Another is redistribution. This refers to traffic changing its destination in response to highway improvements[16]. The majority of toll road forecasting models accommodate trip reassignment but not trip redistribution. This is a weakness. To understand what this means, consider the example below.

Example:

Today I travel to 'x' for work, 'y' for shopping and 'z' for leisure and recreation. A new toll road opens in my area. The forecasting model accommodates the fact that I might now use the toll road to go to 'x', 'y' or 'z' (depending on its relative attractiveness, discussed earlier). However the model will not accommodate the fact that, because of the new road and enhanced accessibility, I might go to 'b' for my shopping, 'c' for my leisure or (over time) might move my working location to 'a'.

Moving away from the fixed trip matrix assumption has proved to be technically challenging. Most forecasters acknowledge the constraint and live with it. Does it matter? Over the long term the answer is undoubtedly 'yes' – but little in practice can be done about it. However it provides a stark reminder that traffic models remain crude and imperfect simplifications of real life and all its complexities.

Having adjusted the matrices' row and column totals, the individual cell values are furnessed to provide new cell values (which

---

[16] Reassignment and redistribution are only two of the changes in trip-making patterns that can take place. Others include trips being made at different times of the day, trips transferring to other modes (eg. bus) and trip generation (the release of suppressed demand). All of these changes – apart from redistribution – can relatively easily be accommodated by traffic modellers.

add up to match the new row and column totals). Now we have a future-year demand matrix. This is assigned to the future-year highway network to provide future flows on links – including the flow on our key link of interest; the toll road.

A number of future-years will be modelled, perhaps at five or ten year intervals, but not all – and models are seldom run for periods beyond 30 years. Interpolation will be used to derive the traffic forecasts for the intervening (non-modelled) years and extrapolation will be used should forecasts be required beyond the 30 year predictive horizon. This raises another important issue for credit analysts. Traffic forecasting focuses on predicting stable long-term trends. It does not accommodate the inevitable year-to-year deviations from these trends which could be significant. Investment-grade transaction structures need to be able to weather short-term fluctuations and departures from expectations, despite what the traffic model may suggest. Transaction structuring that relies too heavily on predictions of smooth and uninterrupted traffic growth fails to reflect the practical limitations of applied forecasting today.

REVENUE FORECASTS

Traffic forecasting involves the modelling of part of a weekday – typically peak period 'time slices' as has been described. Revenue models or, more usually, the revenue line(s) in detailed financial models – tend to require annual or semi-annual inputs. Thus peak period traffic has to be converted to annual (or semi-annual) equivalents and the aggregate tolls generated by this traffic have to be calculated. This two-stage process is not as straightforward as it first may appear – and should be clearly understood by anyone making decisions based on forecasts of toll revenues.

Expansion factors are used to extrapolate from peak period traffic to daily traffic, and then to annual figures – and these annual estimates are very sensitive to the actual expansion factors used. Relatively small and perfectly credible adjustments to expansion factor assumptions can have such a magnified impact on annual traffic (and revenue) calculations, it is beholden upon the traffic modeller to explain and defend the expansion factor assumptions that he/she has made. Suspicions should arise if these calculations are anything other than simple and transparent.

A further complication arises with expansion factors. Should the expansion factors be held constant throughout the forecasting horizon? After all, increasing traffic volumes in the past have changed driver behaviour. To avoid congestion, people leave earlier for work today than they did ten or even five years ago. This is called 'peak spreading' and there is no reason to suggest that it will not continue. So the relationship between, for example, AM peak hour traffic and daily flows in the future could be expected to change. This is not the place for a detailed discussion about peak spreading however any model assumptions made in this regard should be explicit and should be defended in traffic and revenue study reports.

Turning to the financial projections, the relationship between a toll road's traffic and revenue forecasts used to be fairly straightforward;

Revenue = Traffic * Toll

...where Traffic may be divided into a mix of different vehicle categories

...and Toll represents the respective tariffs

Adjustments might be made to take account of any facility-specific discount programmes and for estimates of toll evasion (revenue leakage). However today's toll facilities are becoming increasingly more sophisticated in terms of their tariff schedules – thanks, largely, to the increasing popularity of Electronic Toll Collection (ETC) technologies. In a recent study reviewed by the author, tolls were differentiated by vehicle class, by toll road segment, by direction of travel and by time of day. This complicates the relationship between traffic and revenue considerably. Highly disaggregated demand forecasts are required – in the case above, by vehicle class, by toll road segment, by direction of travel and by time of day – such that these disaggregated demand volumes can be multiplied by their respective tariffs before being consolidated into a single revenue number. And this situation is likely to become more challenging. In parts of the world – notably in the US – variable pricing is being introduced; the price of using a toll road changing dynamically in response to the number of vehicles using it. These developments make it essential for traffic advisers to explain in very clear terms the relationship(s) between traffic and toll tariffs, and the basis of their revenue projections.

KEY MODEL INPUTS: A REVIEW

Most of the inputs into the traffic forecasting process have already been mentioned. To recap, these are summarised below as a checklist – alongside questions which a traffic adviser/study would be expected to have addressed.

- **The Transportation Model**. Which modelling approach/package is used (and why)? How many zones are used and how have these been defined? Which time period(s) are modelled, why and what are the limitations of the approach adopted? What expansion factors are used to derive annual estimates of trips/revenue and how sensitive are the revenue projections to the use of alternative (yet plausible) factors? How is the toll facility represented in the traffic model? Is this a highway-only model, or is multi-modal competition accommodated? Are different vehicle classes used in the model – if so, how have these been defined and why?

- **The Transportation Network**. At what level of detail is the highway network represented and why? How many future-year networks are defined and for which years? How do these networks differ? What certainty exists around any future-year network developments that have been modelled – and the timing of these improvements? Which alternative routes are the more significant sources of competition?

- **Planning Data**. What socio-demographic or land use variables are used in the model and how? What development has been assumed and is it committed or purely speculative? Which data sources have been used and what is their credibility/reliability?

- **Survey Data**. What traffic surveys have been carried out and why? Where? When? What are the sample sizes? What levels of confidence apply to the sampled results? What driver surveys have been carried out and why? Have values of time been calculated? What are they and what level(s) of confidence surround them? Are these values assumed to grow in the future? If so, by how much – and why?

- **Traffic Growth**. What growth rates have been assumed and why? How has growth been incorporated in the forecasting model? What assumptions have been made about ramp-up[17] and why? How sensitive are revenue projections to alternative (yet plausible) growth assumptions?

Each of these inputs (or sets of inputs) should be described in traffic and revenue study reports along with (a) justification for the value(s) adopted, (b) a discussion of how they were used, and (c) indications of the appropriate sensitivity and breakeven tests that had to be conducted – and their results.

TRAFFIC MODELLING: CLOSING REMARKS

The modelling representation of the supply-side of the travel economy – the highway network – was considered at the start of this chapter. Because of the frequent use of GPS-derived cartography, the supply-side is often represented with (literally) military accuracy. It is very important that the users of traffic and revenue forecasts are not seduced by supply-side science into believing that the overall traffic model is more rigorous than it actually is. These models are as strong as their weakest links – and the weakest links inevitably have to do with the 'art' of demand representation and the treatment of demand growth. Good analysts and informed investors focus most of their

---

[17] Ramp-up is the period upon toll road opening characterised by strong growth in usage – from a low base – as travellers become accustomed to the new facility and its features. It may also reflect a protest-period and some initial consumer reluctance to pay tolls. Ramp-up ends when usage of the facility matures, travel patterns stabilise and longer-term trip-making trends become more evident.

critical attention there.

For completeness, Figure 2.5 summarises the traditional toll road traffic and revenue forecasting process in its entirety.

FIGURE 2.5: THE TRAFFIC & REVENUE FORECASTING PROCESS

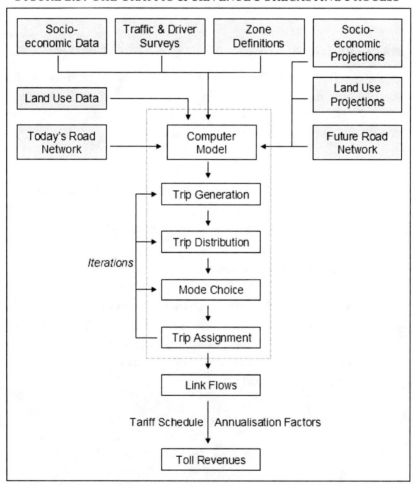

3. TRAFFIC RISK: EMPIRICAL EVIDENCE

THE PREDICTIVE ACCURACY OF TRAFFIC FORECASTING MODELS

Despite the fact that traffic forecasting models have been in use for over 50 years, there is relatively little published about their predictive accuracy. However six research streams (reflecting studies from different parts of the world) merit some attention:

- JP Morgan (1997) – USA.
- Standard & Poor's (2002, 2003, 2004 & 2005) – International.
- Flyvbjerg et al (2005) – International.
- US Transportation Research Board (2006) – USA.
- Vassallo (2007) – Spain.
- Li & Hensher (2009) – Australia.

In this chapter, each of these studies is considered in turn, and their findings and conclusions are summarised. A commentary follows. Building on the study findings, key sources of forecasting error are highlighted and alternative approaches to the assessment of forecasting risk are described.

JP Morgan (1997)

In 1997, the investment bank JP Morgan published the findings from a small-sample review of toll road traffic forecasts[18]. The study examined 14 recently constructed urban toll roads across the United States, comparing actual performance – in this case, toll revenues – with original forecasts. The bank presented its findings as percentages, reflecting the ratio of actual-to-forecast performance. This has the advantage of collapsing the findings from each facility into a single

---

[18] '*Examining Tollroad Feasibility Studies*', Municipal Finance Journal, Vol. 18, No. 1, Spring 1997.

number, with results greater than 100% indicating incidences of forecast under-prediction. There were few results greater than 100%.

In the first year of operations, only one of the 14 toll roads exceeded its revenue prediction. Three of the roads missed the mark by up to 25%. For four of the toll roads, actual revenue was less than 30% of the forecasted equivalent. In response, the bank noted that:

> *"Reducing the uncertainty associated with these forecasts represents one of the major challenges for transportation agencies, traffic consultants, investment bankers and investors."*

Toll road project counterparties still face this major challenge today.

Standard & Poor's (2002, 2003, 2004 & 2005)

In 2002, Standard & Poor's published what was to become one of four annual credit research reports critically examining toll road traffic forecasting accuracy[19]. Over four years, the rating agency compiled data from more than 100 international toll roads, bridges and tunnels allowing for a comparison of forecasts with actual (outturn) traffic volumes. Following the convention adopted by JP Morgan, the rating agency presented its findings as ratios of actual-to-forecast performance – although this time indices rather than percentages were used. An index (ratio) above 1.0 represents under-prediction. In common with JP Morgan's findings, the majority of case studies revealed ratios below 1.0, reflecting the fact that actual traffic volumes using the tolled facilities were systematically lower than their respective forecasts.

Figure 3.1 summarises Standard & Poor's 2005 findings from 104 individual toll road traffic forecasting case studies. The mean of the distribution sits at 0.77 suggesting, on average, over-prediction (optimism-bias) of 20% - 25%. This finding was consistent with conclusions published by the rating agency in its earlier annual reports.

---

[19] '*Traffic Risk in Start-Up Toll Facilities*', Standard & Poor's, September 2002.

FIGURE 3.1: RATIO OF ACTUAL/FORECAST TRAFFIC (S&P)

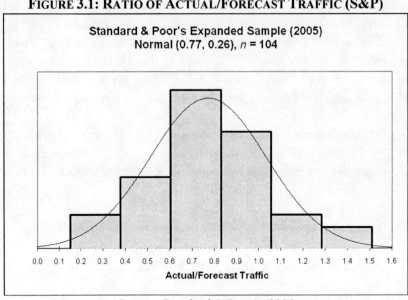

Source: Standard & Poor's, 2005

Initially Standard & Poor's research focused on the analysis of opening-year toll road traffic performance. In later studies[20], the agency extended its scrutiny to consider traffic forecasting performance in subsequent years. Although constrained by data availability, S&P reported that there was no evidence of any improvement in predictive performance after year one. The rating agency attributed much of the revealed optimism bias to the fact that toll road concessions are frequently awarded to bidders predicting the highest traffic and revenue numbers – thus rewarding optimism, not accuracy. This view is supported by Flyvbjerg (discussed later). High revenue projections are also required to support the significant – sometimes aggressive – levels of debt associated with many toll road financings.

Aside from revealing systematic optimism-bias, Standard & Poor's research demonstrates the magnitude of the errors associated with toll road traffic forecasts. The left tail of the distribution presented above represents projects where actual traffic was less than

---

[20] '*Traffic Forecasting Risk Study Update 2005: Through Ramp-Up and Beyond*', Standard & Poor's, August 2005.

20% of that predicted. The right tail shows traffic exceeding predictions by over 50% – however that upside is of more interest to equity rather than fixed income analysts.

The limited space in this guide does not allow for a detailed discussion of all of Standard & Poor's research and results. However their key findings are summarised below:

- Forecasts made on behalf of banks were found to be less optimistic (more conservative) than those prepared for bidders.
- Forecasts made in countries where toll roads had been established for some time were more accurate than those made in jurisdictions new to tolling.
- Complex tariff schedules and payment mechanisms increased the uncertainty surrounding forecasting performance.
- Probability models have a contribution to make – but have to be realistically specified (probability models are discussed later in this chapter).
- Forecasts made for toll-free roads where drivers do not pay at the point of use (including shadow toll roads) share the same error characteristics as those made for user-paid toll roads.
- Forecasts of truck usage were even more unreliable than those made for cars. Standard & Poor's underscores the revenue implication of this finding. Trucks typically represent a small proportion of the traffic mix (commonly less than 10%) but, because of tariff differentials, may contribute over 25% of all project revenues[21].
- Because of aggressive growth assumptions, projects that under-perform in their early years may never catch-up with their original forecasts in later years.

In addition, Standard & Poor's identified common reasons for forecasting accuracy failure in the past. From these, the agency developed a Traffic Risk Index against which projects could be assessed for possible exposure to predictive failure. S&P's Traffic Risk Index is discussed further in Chapter 4.

---

[21] Trucks on some North American toll roads – the Pennsylvania Turnpike, for example – contribute up to 50% of project revenues.

Flyvbjerg et al (2005)

In 2005, Flyvbjerg et al published the results from a large-sample survey of road and rail demand forecasting performance[22]. In terms of road traffic, the authors focused outside the toll road sector on regular (toll-free) roads – however a number of their findings are relevant here. Flyvbjerg's analysis suggested that

- Accuracy in traffic forecasting has shown no improvement over the past 30 years.
- For half of the road projects analysed, the difference between actual and forecasted traffic was over +/- 20%.
- For a quarter of the road projects, the difference was over +/- 40%.

Standard & Poor's later published a comparative analysis of their (toll road) findings against Flyvbjerg's (free road) results. This analysis suggested that the systematic tendency towards optimism bias demonstrated from the toll road research was not replicated in the free road dataset. Toll-free road forecasts had an equal chance of under/ over-prediction. However, in terms of predictive error, the toll road and free road forecasts behaved similarly, showing very wide error ranges.

US Transportation Research Board (2006)

As part of its National Cooperative Highway Research Program, in 2006 the US Transportation Research Board (TRB) published a 'synthesis of highway practice' looking specifically at toll road demand and revenue studies. Among other things, this synthesis reported actual toll revenues as a percentage of those forecasted for 26 US toll facilities over their first five years of operations. Actual revenue turned out to lie 30% - 40% below that predicted. Out of 104 separate observations, only 13 of the outturn revenue figures were within +/- 10% (and only one-third fell within +/- 25%) of the projected revenues.

---

[22] '*How (In)accurate are Demand Forecasts in Public Works Projects?*', Journal of the American Planning Association, Vol.71, No. 2, Spring 2005.

Vassallo (2007)

In 2007, Vassallo published the results from a small-sample study of toll road forecasts in Spain[23]. Contrary to S&P's findings, the author reports that – in his sample – traffic prediction accuracy improved after year one. However, the general trend he reports was that there was a clear bias towards the over-estimation of traffic. Vassallo states that the magnitude of this over-estimation was in line with, although slightly above, S&P's earlier findings (+35%).

Li & Hensher (2009)

The most recent contribution to the literature focuses attention on the Australian toll road sector[24]. Li & Hensher examined 13 toll roads, bridges and tunnels in Sydney, Melbourne and Brisbane. Comparative (actual versus forecast) traffic figures are reported for ten of the facilities, although the dataset in terms of annual comparative data for each road is incomplete. Year-one comparisons were available for five roads, however, and these demonstrated that forecasted traffic volumes were 45% greater than outturn figures. The authors comment that *"This is significantly higher than the numbers quoted by Standard & Poor's"*.

In line with Vassallo, Li & Hensher report some gradual improvements in forecasting performance after the first year of project operations. One road evolved from underperformance of 33% in Year 1 to over-performance by 3% nine years later. Outturn traffic on another improved from 48% of the forecast to 55% over a three year period – a slow recovery from dismal opening-year performance. In conclusion, the authors report that *"Actual toll road traffic may adjust to the forecast however this could take a long period of time"*, adding that another toll road was still 19% lower than forecasts after six years of operations.

---

[23] '*Why Traffic Forecasts in PPP Contracts are Often Overestimated*', EIB University Research Sponsorship Programme, EIB, Luxembourg, 2007.
[24] '*Toll Roads in Australia*', Institute of Transport and Logistics Studies, University of Sydney, 2009.

EMPIRICAL EVIDENCE – COMMENTARY

The empirical evidence on toll road traffic and revenue forecasting performance is clear and consistent, and should send three stark warnings to analysts: errors are common, they are commonly large and over-prediction – optimism-bias – is a consistent theme. The TRB sample demonstrated that two-thirds of revenue forecasts were off-target by more than 25%. This is a striking finding in terms of predictive accuracy. It is more worrying from a credit perspective to note that the vast majority (>90%) of these errors were over-predictions. Very few observations (only 5 out of 105) reflected circumstances under which toll revenues had been under-predicted by more than 25%!

This reflects the reality of state-of-the-practice toll road forecasting. How can an analyst detect whether or not a project being reviewed is particularly exposed to error or bias? The remainder of this guide addresses this central question. A useful starting place is to review the most common sources of error that have caused predictive failure in the past so that credit analysts can be alert for early warning signs.

COMMON SOURCES OF FORECASTING ERROR

Error Drivers

As a result of their four years of investigations into toll road traffic forecasts, Standard & Poor's compiled a list of common sources of predictive error. Their top ten sources are summarised below (no hierarchy of importance is inferred).

High Toll Tariffs

High toll tariffs were identified by the rating agency as a recurring source of forecasting error. This refers to tariffs sitting outside the rates per mile (or per kilometre) usually observed – and the associated consumer response which is not well understood. High toll tariffs are sometimes charged on new urban tolled facilities to recover the significant up-front capital costs associated with demolition and construction works in built-up areas. The rating agency also pointed out that the response of frequent users (commuters, for example) to high toll tariffs has been overstated in the past.

Future Land Use Scenarios or Economic Performance that did not Transpire

Future traffic growth estimates are predicated on assumptions about how land use around toll facilities will develop in the future. Some toll roads in North America, for example, fell well short of their traffic expectations due to unanticipated and significant down-scaling of local commercial and residential development. Similarly, traffic growth often depends upon key assumptions about future economic performance in a study area. If economic performance falls short of expectations, toll road traffic volumes may not grow as anticipated – or at all.

Time Savings Less than Anticipated

If drivers do not realise or perceive the time-saving benefits of using toll facilities – particularly on short urban facilities – traffic numbers and revenues are unlikely to match expectations. Analysts need to ensure that the potential for time savings to be eroded are fully understood and are factored into their assessments. Toll roads terminating in downtown areas may cause delays to drivers who have saved time travelling on the facility only to have to queue to re-join the busy toll-free network. This phenomenon is known as 'hurry up and wait'.

Improvement to Competitive (toll-free) Routes

Some toll road concession agreements grant exclusivity to the concessionaire – providing them with protection from competition. Others contain undertakings that the attractiveness of competing roads will be degraded, or provide for compensation to be paid should new competing routes abstract revenues from the tolled facility. However many more agreements are silent on the competitive context within which toll roads operate (today and in the future) – leaving the roads exposed to competition. This risk needs to be well understood as it can lead to material cash flow impairment over which the concessionaire has little or no control.

Less Usage by Trucks

The unreliability of truck forecasts combined with the fact that they are often key revenue contributors underscores the importance of understanding the extent to which toll road cash flows rely on trucking demand. Truckers – particularly owner/drivers – often avoid toll roads; especially when they first open. This protest period can be deep and more protracted than anticipated, even under downside sensitivity tests. The UK's M6 Toll is a good example of a road carrying fewer trucks than originally predicted although it is far from alone in that regard. Revenue forecasts were subsequently rebased to take account of actual truck usage.

Less Off-Peak or Weekend Traffic

Traffic models usually simulate peak period traffic conditions. Assumptions are made about the relationship between peak and off-peak periods, and these assumptions are carried forward to the calculation of aggregate (full-day or full-year) demand. However peak periods are characterised by time-sensitive trip purposes such as commuting, when drivers experience heavily congested road conditions and attach high values to travel time savings. Outside these peak periods, journeys (for shopping or leisure) become less time-critical, networks become less congested and drivers may be less willing to pay for (quite commonly) relatively small time savings. Analysts need to understand the peak/off-peak composition of toll revenues and ensure that assumptions about weekday off-peak or weekend toll road travel behaviour are well grounded.

Complexity of the Toll Tariff Schedule

The development and ever-more widespread application of electronic toll collection technologies enables toll road operators or procuring agencies to become quite sophisticated in terms of their pricing strategies. In the past, drivers typically paid a simple flat or distance-related rate to travel the length of a toll road. Today, that rate may vary by section of road, direction of travel, time of day, day of week, season of the year and, dynamically, according to the level of congestion. Pricing has become more sophisticated and so too have the payment options available to toll road customers. Drivers may be less conscious of the exact amount paid – and behave differently – if billed via credit card account on a monthly basis. All of this compounds the traffic forecasting challenge. Traffic models have to be applied at a more granular level so that the various cash flow components can be estimated before being aggregated. Analysts should note that this moves away from the preference, noted at the outset, for a simple traffic story that accords with intuition.

Under-Estimation of Ramp-Up

Ramp-up is the period upon project opening when drivers are still familiarising themselves and experimenting with the new facility. It is commonly characterised by strong growth from a low base. It ends when travel patterns mature into a steady-state and growth settles into a longer-term trend. Anticipating the shape and duration of a ramp-up profile is acknowledged by many to be one of the most difficult challenges faced by traffic forecasters. Many simply impose a 'guesstimated' profile (such as 70%, 90%, 100% over three years) with little empirical justification. An extended discussion of ramp-up lies beyond the remit of this guide. However it should be noted that, particularly on greenfield projects, ramp-up can take considerably longer than anticipated leading to depressed cash flows in the financially-sensitive early years of project operations. Given the uncertainty, it would seem sensible to conduct rigorous sensitivity tests – assessing the resilience of the financial model to alternative ramp-up assumptions.

Miscalculation of Value(s) of Travel Time Savings

As a concept, the value of travel time savings (VTTS) lies at the heart of all toll road traffic forecasting models. However values of time savings vary among individuals and, indeed, vary for the same individual based on factors such as journey purpose. Our value of time saved when travelling to an airport to catch a flight will be much higher than when we are taking a scenic drive on vacation. Toll road traffic forecasting reports need to explain what values of time savings have been used in models, how they have been estimated and how they have been applied – and provide strong justification in each case.

Long-Term Forecasts Sensitive to GDP Assumptions

Because of the long forecasting horizons, typically stretching 30 years or beyond, the cumulative impact of relatively small differences in the assumptions made about GDP or traffic growth rates can turn out to be considerable. This is illustrated in Figure 3.2. At the end of the forecasting horizon, traffic tracking a 3% growth rate is around half of that calculated under the 5% growth rate scenario. Not many toll road financial models could withstand a 50% traffic 'haircut'.

FIGURE 3.2: LONG-TERM FORECAST SENSITIVITY

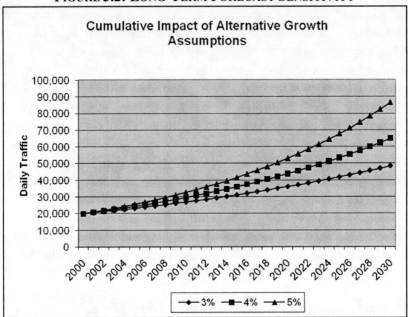

OTHER SOURCES OF FORECASTING ERROR

Aside from the work by Standard & Poor's, there is little in the literature to provide guidance about the potential sources of traffic forecasting error. The Flyvbjerg research identified accuracy problems stemming from the use of survey data and planning variables that were out-of-date. In common with S&P's findings, Flyvbjerg also points to land use scenarios that had failed to crystallise as anticipated.

More generally, Flyvbjerg's work has focussed, not on error, but on optimism-bias[25]. He warns about what he terms *"strategic misrepresentation"*[26]; parties to a transaction deliberately talking-up the numbers in support of some action or achieve a specific objective (such as raising a significant volume of debt and/or winning a bidding competition for a toll road concession).

In 2002, a study by Muller and Buono[27] examined a number of US toll road forecasts with a view to identifying any relationships between forecasting performance and the attributes of the toll roads themselves. Their findings are summarised in Table 3.1. There is considerable consistency between the Muller and Buono findings and the results from the Standard & Poor's research. Muller and Buono linked poor forecasting performance with roads developed to stimulate economic activity (rather than meet existing demand) and roads with high tolls – whereas more reliable forecasting performance was observed for toll roads in busy, high income corridors with good connectivity to the rest of the highway network.

The error drivers summarised earlier – many of which are reflected in Table 3.1 – were carried forward by Standard & Poor's into the compilation of their Traffic Risk Index (discussed later).

---

[25] *'Megaprojects and Risk: An Anatomy of Ambition'*, B Flyvbjerg et al, Cambridge University Press, 2003.

[26] Giglio (1998) refers to this phenomenon as *"intellectual dishonesty"*.

[27] *'Start-Up Toll Roads: Separating Winners from Losers'*, Municipal Credit Monitor, JP Morgan, New York, 2002.

TABLE 3.1: FORECAST PERFORMANCE & ROAD CHARACTERISTICS

Forecast Performance	Toll Road Characteristics
Actual performance equalled or exceeded forecasts	Well-developed urban/suburban part of large metropolitan area
	High corridor income
	Substantial corridor traffic
	High value of travel time savings
	Good connections to facility
	No competitive non-tolled alternatives
	Modest projected traffic growth
Actual performance between 61% and 67% of forecast	Less-established traffic patterns
	Less integral to the existing network
	These were partial beltways
	Usually serving above-average income areas but with less-established development patterns
	Further from employment centres
	Moderate to high toll rates (although usage inelastic because drivers already accustomed to paying tolls)
Actual performance between 51% and 60% of forecast	Corridors with more developed or already established traffic patterns
	Usually constructed in large metropolitan areas or active tourist areas
	'Solid' projected time savings
	Moderate projected revenue growth
Actual performance between 29% and 50% of forecast	Specific traffic generator serving as a project basis (eg. airport)
	Located in undeveloped area
	Toll road expected to stimulate development
	High revenue growth rates
	Assumed periodic toll rate increases

Source: Adapted from Muller and Buono (2002)

APPROACHES TO MODELLING RISK

Sensitivity Tests and Scenario Analysis

Experienced analysts have adapted to the unreliability of the traffic forecasting process in ways that bring sensitivity testing and scenario analysis centre-stage. Before rushing into sensitivity tests, however, we need to understand – and, ideally, secure broad buy-into – what we are sensitising. This brings us to the base or central case traffic forecasts.

The purpose of the base case is to reflect what we believe is the most likely future scenario. At this stage, attempts to overlay subjective impressions of how we would prefer some of the input variables to be sized are unhelpful and serve to confuse. Our appetite for or aversion to risk should not find expression in a base case.

Base case traffic forecasts may be accompanied by an upside (equity) case and a downside (debt) case. Equity considerations lie beyond the focus of this guide. A downside case (sometimes labelled 'the bank case') results from scenario analysis – a series of individual sensitivity tests brought together as a collective (the scenario). This is where our risk appetite should be reflected; in the variables selected for sensitising and the extent to which they are sensitised. Remember, however, a downside case only achieves its objectives if it is the downside of a base case which retains credibility.

Probabilistic Modelling

With sensitivity tests, the traffic modeller adopts a parameter value that differs from that used in the base case and the impact on key outputs (usually traffic flows along the tolled link in the highway network) are examined. With scenario analysis, a number of sensitivity tests are combined and are run together. In both cases, all of the input variables are point estimates (eg. a value of time saved of €10/hour, or GDP growth of 2.5% per annum). The model assumes that there is only one possible value for each of the variables, assumes that the forecaster knows what that value is and assumes that the forecaster is correct! Such a model is known as a deterministic model.

An alternative approach is to use a probabilistic model. The most common form is the Monte Carlo simulation model. A number of traffic consultancies advocate the use of Monte Carlo simulation models for toll road traffic and revenue forecasting. These models do not use point estimates. Instead they use ranges and likelihoods. Say that GDP had grown between 1% and 4% per annum over the last 20 years, that it had averaged 2.5% per annum and you believe that the future will be similar to the past (usually the biggest and most dangerous assumption in the traffic model). A probabilistic model enables the forecaster to capture this information. GDP growth would be specified as:

Minimum Value	Most Likely	Maximum Value
1.0%	2.5%	4.0%

This defines a triangular distribution for GDP growth, as shown in Figure 3.3.

FIGURE 3.3: TRIANGULAR DISTRIBUTION (1, 2.5, 4)

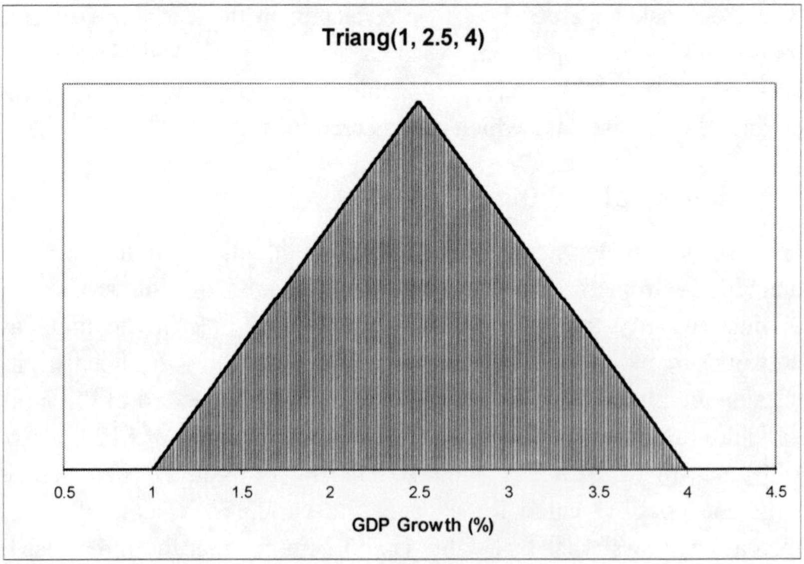

Source: @RISK (http://www.palisade.com/)

Probabilistic models can become very sophisticated. In the deterministic model discussed earlier, we assumed that the value of time savings was €10/hour. Figure 3.4 below shows the results of assuming that values of time savings follow a different (this time, lognormal) distribution[28]. The average value of time saved is still €10/hour but some people have lower values of time whereas others have much higher values of time – hence the positive skew (the long right-hand tail).

FIGURE 3.4: LOGNORMAL DISTRIBUTION (10, 5)

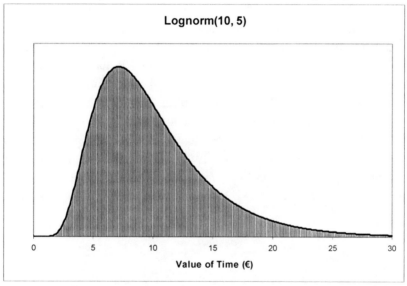

Source: @RISK (http://www.palisade.com/)

The detail of probabilistic modelling remains unimportant here. It is the concept of re-casting point estimates as probabilities (or, more accurately, probability distribution functions) that is of note. However some care needs to be taken with probability models:

- The traffic modeller has to define which variables to cast as probabilities (and should be able to justify this).

---

[28] As income levels are commonly observed to be log-normally distributed, a lognormal distribution is often suggested for values of travel time savings.

- The traffic modeller has to define which probability distribution functions to use (and should be able to justify them).

Some variables may interact with each other so, in addition, the modeller needs to define (a) which variables interact, and (b) the nature of that interaction (co-variance). As above, their reasoning should be justifiable.

Probabilistic models are not a substitute for traditional traffic models. They are an extension of them. In practice, traffic forecasters take the outputs from traditional traffic models and use them as inputs into probabilistic models. Effectively, they model the model.

As probabilities substitute for point estimate inputs in a Monte Carlo simulation model, the model's outputs are similarly presented as probabilities or ranges. This can be very useful in terms of indicating the uncertainty surrounding, say, traffic volumes using a toll road in 2015. However the GIGO adage applies here (garbage in, garbage out). A traffic forecaster using unrealistically narrow ranges for selected input variables will produce an unrealistically narrow range for the output (traffic usage in 2015). This will infer a degree of precision and certainty in their results that is simply unsupported by the predictive performance evidence reviewed earlier.

4. *WHAT TO LOOK FOR IN A TRAFFIC & REVENUE STUDY*

INTRODUCTION

This final chapter is divided into five short sections. The first introduces a set of analytical techniques which can be used to examine toll road traffic and revenue forecasts from alternative perspectives. The second suggests ways in which traffic advisers could better present the results of their research specifically for an investor audience. Acknowledging that there may be pressure to inflate toll road traffic and revenue forecasts under certain circumstances, the third section looks at ways in which this can be achieved – tricks for credit analysts to remain alert to. The fourth section contains a review checklist; quick questions which analysts can ask themselves to check their understanding of any toll road forecasting study. Finally, conclusions are drawn about toll road traffic forecasting today – and in the future – and the implications that flow for investment-grade transaction structuring are considered.

ALTERNATIVE ANALYTICAL APPROACHES

Up to this point the focus has been on the detail behind traffic modelling and the preparation of revenue forecasts so that the readers of demand study reports can better understand the material presented to them. It is instructive, however, to approach toll road traffic and revenue forecasts from different perspectives. Different perspectives aid the report reader's understanding and can act as a form of intuitive 'sense check'. Five alternative approaches are set out below for analysts to consider:

- Keeping it simple,
- Deconstruction and reconstruction,
- Critical point analysis,
- Incremental analysis,

- Use of the Traffic Risk Index.

Keeping It Simple

Keeping it simple refers to stripping away much of the often-confusing detail contained in traffic and revenue study reports and concentrating on the fundamentals. Collapse the road network to a simplified stick-diagram, for example – as shown in Figure 4.1.

FIGURE 4.1: STICK DIAGRAM OF KEY HIGHWAY LINKS

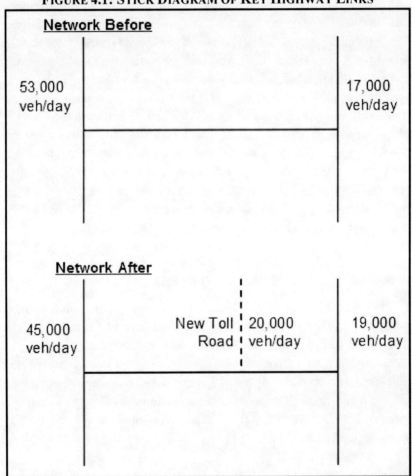

From Figure 4.1 it can be seen that the total north-south movement is 70,000 vehicles/day before the construction of the new toll road and 84,000 vehicles/day afterwards. This needs to be explained. It might be because of background traffic growth or because of induced traffic[29] – or some combination thereof. Notwithstanding, the simple stick representation highlights the issue and prompts the question. Similarly, we can see that the new toll road captures around 25% of total corridor traffic (20,000/84,000). Is this reasonable? What evidence has the traffic adviser presented – perhaps from comparable schemes – in support of this high capture rate? A simple stick representation of the toll road of interest set within the context of its key competing links (showing daily traffic volumes) is a useful way of enhancing your understanding of how travellers are predicted to respond to the new facility – and you can ask yourself, *"Does this make sense?"*.

Sticking with the keep it simple philosophy, tabulate all of the traffic adviser's modelling and forecasting assumptions on a single sheet of paper. Better still, get them to do this! Table 4.1 on the following page presents a template. Many traffic and revenue study reports fail to make all of their underpinning assumptions clear – or contain references to them scattered across different pages. This is unhelpful. Consolidating them on one sheet focuses attention on the factors driving the forecasts; prompting questions about any assumptions supported by little, weak or no evidence. The list of assumptions can also be compared to the sensitivity tests described in the report to see if the most appropriate sensitivities have been conducted – not just those hand-picked by the traffic adviser.

The keep it simple philosophy builds on the notion introduced at the very beginning of this guide – that simple traffic stories that accord with intuition are most likely to attract the broadest buy-in. Stories that require elaborate explanations or which, ultimately, remain a mystery may be credible yet should be treated very cautiously by credit analysts.

---

[29] Construction of a new highway facility may, by itself, increase the amount of trip-making in an area. That increase is said to have been induced by the network improvement – however there is limited empirical data about the precise magnitude of induced traffic in given circumstances.

TABLE 4.1: KEY MODELLING ASSUMPTIONS

Variable	Assumption	Justification/Source/ Comments
General		
Modelling software package		
Modelled time period(s)		
Zone definitions		
Base year		
Scheme opening year		
Number of vehicle classes		
Number of journey purposes		
Planning Variables		
Population growth		
Households growth		
Employment growth		
GDP growth		
Income growth		
Car ownership growth		
Development assumptions		
Network Variables		
Capacity/lane		
Capacity growth		
Speed limits		
Traffic/Driver Variables		
Toll tariff (eg. cents/mile)		
Toll tariff escalation		
Value(s) of time		
Value of time escalation		
ETC penetration		
ETC growth		

ETC bonus		
ETC discounts/violations		
Motorway bonus		
Induced traffic		
Traffic growth (short term)		
Traffic growth (long term)		
Annualisation/Revenue Variables		
Expansion factors		
Peak-hour spreading		
Tariff schedule		
Tariff escalation		
Tariff elasticity		
Ramp-up profile		
Future year(s) modelled		
Revenue growth (short term)		
Revenue growth (long term)		

Some of these variables are model outputs (as opposed to inputs), however it is instructive to have them summarised – and justified – in a single table. This list is not exclusive. Traffic advisers should tailor the table to reflect the variables used and assumptions made in particular circumstances. Justification should also be provided for those assumptions that remain constant (and those that change) in future years.

Deconstruct and Reconstruct

The objective behind deconstruct-and-reconstruct is to dig into the forecast numbers to identify the key contributors to the overall revenue stream. The technique is best illustrated by example.

A toll road is forecasted to carry 35,000 vehicles/day shortly after opening. 20,000 vehicles will transfer (re-assign) from a highly congested, sub-standard, toll-free facility running parallel to the new toll road. 10,000 will transfer from other local roads in the area, and 5,000 will transfer from two motorways some distance from the new road. The new road will generate annual revenues of €10m. The financial model shows that the project needs to generate €7.5m to meet debt servicing obligations and cover operating costs.

Analysts are concerned about some of the assumptions behind the forecasts and feel that there is particular uncertainty about how many drivers will transfer from the two distant motorways (and, to a lesser extent, from the local road network). A session with the traffic consultants suggests that different levels of confidence can be attributed to the different sources of transfer traffic, albeit subjectively (see Table 4.2).

TABLE 4.2: DECONSTRUCTION & RECONSTRUCTION

Traffic Source	Total Traffic per Day	Confidence	Effective Traffic per Day
Parallel Road	20,000	100%	20,000
Local Roads	10,000	70%	7,000
Motorways	5,000	0%	0
Total			27,000

By deconstructing the traffic flow and reconstructing (taking account of unknowns, uncertainties, risk aversion or unease), the analytical team becomes comfortable with traffic volumes around 27,000/day. As 27,000 vehicles/day generates annual revenues above the breakeven threshold (€7.5m), credit committee buys-into the revenue-generating characteristics of the toll road and can turn its attention to other risks and risk-mitigating features of the transaction.

This is a simple example. All the analysts saw at the outset was the forecast of 35,000 vehicles/day. By digging into the numbers and identifying key contributors to the overall revenue steam, they were able to develop their understanding. Essentially they back-solved the problem by asking:

(a) what do we need, and

(b) what will it take to get us there?

Traffic consultants will not always present their results in this form as they may have limited insight into the answer to question (a).

Critical Point Analysis

If you plot toll road traffic forecasts in time, many of the results will look similar to the profile illustrated in Figure 4.2.

FIGURE 4.2: CRITICAL POINT ANALYSIS

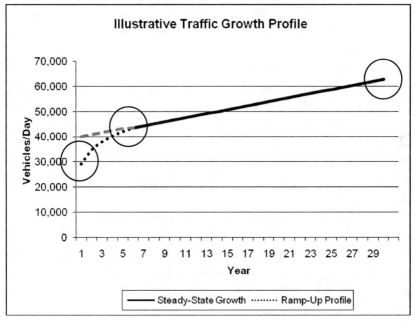

The three circles overlaid on Figure 4.2 represent critical points and traffic forecasters can be asked to reformulate their arguments to support these critical points. Working backwards (from right to left):

- What is the justification for the long-term (steady-state) growth trend?
- What is the justification for the ramp-up profile?
- What is the justification for the opening-year volume?

Again this is simply looking at toll road traffic forecasts from an alternative perspective – but these three questions can provide an insightful agenda for discussions between the users and the producers of traffic forecasts.

Incremental Analysis

It is usual for traffic and revenue reports to present forecasts for the opening of a new tolled facility (or the extension of an existing one) at some future date. The opening year projections reflect a combination of impacts: background traffic growth over the intervening years, the demand associated with the network enhancement and the imposition of tolls. Isolating these impacts to better understand their contribution – individually and collectively – can prove to be instructive. This is the basis of incremental analysis.

The traffic adviser can model the toll road as if it was open today, for example. This allows the impact of the network improvement (the new road) to be isolated from the impacts of various growth assumptions. Do the results make sense? Similarly, the toll can be switched on or off in the model, isolating the impact associated with tolling from that associated with the new link. Again, do the results make sense?

Although purely hypothetical, incremental analysis can be used to understand the important transition period (and the transitioning influences at work) between today and the year of scheme opening. This can be particularly valuable when opening-year usage is predicted to be high.

Standard & Poor's Traffic Risk Index

S&P's Traffic Risk Index was introduced earlier and is presented in full in Appendix A. It is a comprehensive, empirically-derived checklist of toll road features mapped against a subjective ten-point scale. The higher the score against this scale, the more potentially exposed the project is to forecasting risk and uncertainty. At a simple level, the Index can be used as a list of issues for the analyst (or the analyst together with their traffic consultant) to run through to check their understanding of a project and that they have not overlooked any factors which need to be considered.

At a more sophisticated level, scoring can be used. This is illustrated in Appendices B and C. In Appendix B, horizontal bars are used to represent lender exposure to particular risks. In Appendix C, risk scores are supported by comments explaining the rationale underpinning the scores. Both approaches can be used to highlight issues which require further investigation or analysis – even to the point of looking to renegotiate contractual terms regarding these risks, re-pricing them or laying them off to third parties (insurers for example).

This is not to say that all of the risks that attract low scores are unimportant. However this simple risk register – on a single sheet of paper – highlights key project risks requiring particular attention. It is logical and promotes analytical consistency in terms of ensuring that different projects – perhaps the responsibility of different credit analysts or teams – are evaluated similarly and can be compared against common benchmarks.

BEST PRACTICE REPORTING

It may seem strange that the issue of best practice (in terms of reporting the results from a traffic and revenue study) should be included in a guide for the *users* of forecasts. Surely these suggestions should be directed at the forecasters themselves? Best practice is considered here because:

- It enables the readers of forecasting reports to consider how a particular report they are reviewing departs from best practice – and may prompt questions about why?
- There is often a dialogue between report readers and writers, during which it may be insightful to consider some of the issues mentioned below.
- Users of this guide may commission traffic and revenue studies in the future (or may have an input into their terms of reference) and, in that context, best practice guidance could be useful.

There are a number of issues that could be considered to be best practice in terms of conducting a toll road traffic and revenue study and, specifically, reporting its results. Some key issues are considered below.

Understanding and Communicating the Commercial Proposition

Too many traffic and revenue study reports launch into swathes of technical detail without pausing to provide a clear description of the product (the toll facility), the product offering (time savings, reliable travel times, uncongested travel etc.) and the likely consumer response. It has already been pointed out that a simple, intuitively-appealing traffic story is the most powerful tool in terms of securing broad buy-in to the commercial proposition that a toll road represents. Credit analysts will be required to discuss candidate projects with colleagues and present them to credit committees. Traffic and revenue reports should be written in ways that facilitate that communication and concise/accurate presentations by non-technical third-parties.

Base Case Assumptions & Justifications

Base case assumptions should be consolidated in a single table in a traffic and revenue study report. Robust justification should be provided in support of these assumptions. It is helpful if the traffic forecaster can comment, not only upon why particular assumptions were made, but also why others were rejected. These arguments are strengthened considerably when empirical evidence is provided in support.

Some of the forecaster's assumptions may rely upon a continuation of historical trends (eg. GDP has grown at an average of 2% per annum for the last 20 years). Some forecasters place the onus on the report's audience to suggest why such trends would not continue into the future. This is poor. The onus is clearly on the forecaster to explain why such trends should be expected to continue, unchanged in shape or form, well into the future.

It is also useful for the forecaster to critique his or her own work. Better than anyone, they know the limitations of their research[30] and the approaches used, and they know where the residual uncertainties lie. These should be shared, upfront, with the report's audience – rather than having to rely upon later cross-examination. The central

---

[30] Most traffic surveys rely upon sampling for example, and this places limitations on later results.

purpose of a good traffic and revenue study report is not to state a position and then staunchly defend it. Good reports set out to communicate information and share expertise such that informed discussion, debate and understanding is promoted.

Reporting Balance

Too many traffic and revenue study reports are front-end loaded in the sense that perhaps three-quarters of the text is devoted to calibration of the base year model (and all the preparatory work that had to be conducted in advance). A calibrated base year model is not the end of an important process. It's the beginning of one. Much of the preparatory work – and the technical detail that goes along with it – could usefully be presented as report appendices. Model calibration is important, although it is difficult to imagine that the leading consultancies in this field would struggle to produce calibrated base year traffic models; especially if they limit themselves to peak-period modelling. It is what happens once the model is calibrated that is the primary focus for the credit analyst.

In terms of reporting balance, a suggested Table of Contents for a toll road traffic and revenue study specifically prepared for investor scrutiny is presented in Appendix D. This is not a definitive prescription – it is simply an illustration. A concise, digestible report is recommended of around 50 pages; 20 of which focus post-calibration on the forecasts themselves and their interpretation, sensitivity testing and scenario analysis. Sensitivity testing is critical in terms of understanding the strength and resilience of project cash flows. It needs to be conducted intelligently, however, not simply by changing some variables by 10% to see what happens. The forecaster should justify (a) which variables need to be sensitised, (b) why and (c) by how much. The output from sensitivity testing should be information, not just data. What the results mean is more important than what the results are.

The Role of Peer Reviews

Having a peer review conducted of a traffic and revenue study can be a very useful way for the non-technical audience to get up-to-speed with the key analytical issues quickly. Peer reviews are commonplace in the

United States but have yet to be widely adopted elsewhere – although independent due diligence may fulfil some of their functions. However due diligence commissions often result in desk-top reviews whereas there is more interaction between the original traffic consultant and their reviewer under the peer review regime.

HOW TO INFLATE FORECASTS

The evaluation criteria used to award many of today's privately-financed toll road concessions focus on maximising income (or minimising expenditure) for government procuring agencies. In bidding competitions the evaluation criteria are generally published, establishing the 'rules of the game' from the outset. Bidders are incentivised to develop strategies which best respond to the criteria – framing their bids in the best possible light and maximising their chance of winning the competition. Under such circumstances, traffic and revenue forecasts are bound to attract considerable attention.

Bidding strategy success and the ability to raise significant quantities of debt often rely on strong projections of demand; even beyond credibility in situations where the short-term benefits of winning are perceived to overshadow any possible longer-term costs. This is particularly true when profits are front-loaded or in cases where, for practical or reputational reasons, procuring agencies may be open to subsequent contractual renegotiation. In short, the procurement process in general – and bid evaluation criteria specifically – reward high traffic and revenue forecasts, not accurate ones. This places asymmetric pressure on traffic advisers in terms of the outputs from their forecasting models. In that context, the following paragraphs summarise 21 ways in which toll road traffic and revenue projections can be inflated – tricks for investors and credit analysts to watch out for.

1. Flatter the Asset

The representation of a toll road in a traffic model may be flattered in various ways. An incomplete treatment of the delays that drivers experience at toll collection stations or upon leaving the toll road (and re-joining a congested toll-free network) makes the toll road more attractive to potential users. So does exaggerating the capacity per lane. Traffic modellers commonly employ assumptions about how the capacity of a toll facility will actually increase in future years despite its geometry and configuration remaining unchanged! This is supposed to reflect that fact that driver behaviour adapts over time – in terms of following-distance tolerance – such that the 'effective' capacity of a road will increase. Naturally, this improves the attractiveness of the asset. Evidence should be provided by traffic advisers to support such assumptions if they are to be incorporated in base case traffic models.

An alternative approach is to impair the competitive landscape. The competitive position of a toll road will appear to be strong in circumstances where the alternative facilities offer particularly poor levels of service to users. This can be achieved by degrading a competing route's capacity through the use of punitive speed/flow relationships or speed limits, or by over-emphasising delays (such as those experienced by drivers at signalised intersections). It can also be achieved by over-simplifying the competitive context – ignoring important rat-runs in an urban network or by neglecting the potential for competition from other roads or transportation modes in the future.

2. Cherry-Pick your Planning Variables

The future-year socio-demographic and planning variables that are used by traffic models are commonly presented as ranges. Consistent selection of variables from the upper ends of these ranges will, all things being equal, place upward pressure on the traffic numbers. This is one of the reasons why all of a model's input assumptions should be tabulated on a single sheet and justified – with supporting evidence being provided by the traffic adviser.

A variation on this theme is the use of planning variables designed to achieve particular political objectives. A recent report reviewed talked of *"planning targets"*. These seemingly independent and unbiased variables – such as projections of population – may be the basis upon which the state allocates funds to regional governments. Thus there are incentives for the producers of these planning forecasts to inflate their own projections which, in turn, can be used to pump-up the traffic numbers. Understanding the source(s) of these 'independent' socio-demographic and planning variables can help to mitigate this risk. Presenting alternative planning forecasts from different public and private sector sources also provides some comfort to credit analysts and investors.

3. Judiciously 'Identify' the Historical Trend

With a time series of data – such as traffic or toll revenue – it is often possible to isolate different trends by carefully selecting the period to be analysed. Determine what story needs to be told and then find the data to support it. Was the historical growth trend 5% per annum, or 7% or 3%?

Figure 4.3 shows the historical time series of revenue miles from the Pennsylvania Turnpike in the US. Over the period from opening, 1941, to 2006 the compound annual growth rate was 5% per annum. From 1952 to 2006 the rate was only 3%. However, in terms of supporting high traffic forecasts, from 1943 to 2006 the rate was a very useful 7%. These different growth rates are all derived from the same historical data set – just different parts of it.

FIGURE 4.3: TIME SERIES OF REVENUE MILES ON THE PENNSYLVANIA TURNPIKE

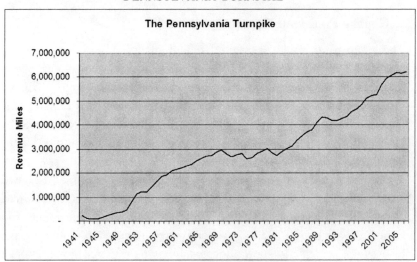

Source: www.paturnpike.com

4. Selectively Apply and/or Report Growth Factors

Traffic and revenue study reports commonly provide area-wide statistics in support of their forecasts. A report might state that, across the study area as a whole, from 2010 to 2030, average population growth of 1.2% per annum is predicted. This appears reasonable – possibly even conservative. But what about the distribution of this growth? If the model is specified such that most of the population growth is anticipated to take place in zones adjacent to or that feed the toll road, it would be no surprise to find high traffic growth rates resulting on the asset itself – certainly higher than 1.2% per annum!

5. The Future Will Look Exactly Like the Past

Some toll road forecasts are made against a backdrop of strong historical traffic growth trends. Why should such trends continue unabated for the next 25-30 years or beyond? And what about historical relationships – such as the elasticity between GDP growth and traffic growth? Why should this relationship remain constant throughout the forecasting horizon? These are for the traffic forecaster to justify – particularly if senior debt accretes or debt amortisation schedules are back-ended. In the absence of solid justification, base case forecasts should be adjusted accordingly to reflect the increasing uncertainty associated with long-range projections and sensitivity tests should be used to evaluate the impact of key relationships which could change in the future.

6. The Future Will Look Nothing Like the Past

A recent traffic and revenue study reviewed by the author demonstrated clearly, with good evidential support, that historical traffic growth across the study area had neither been strong nor consistent. Along some key corridors traffic volumes had been declining. Yet the future, according to the traffic forecasts, was one of strong, sustained growth. No explanation was provided for this dramatic disconnect between the past and the future. At best this hints of model-blindness. The traffic adviser has been engrossed in the mechanics of model building to the extent that they become blind to the credibility of the model outputs. Other symptoms of possible model blindness recently noted include low growth scenarios that resulted in traffic and revenue projections above the base case and severe downside sensitivity tests that had little impact on project revenues. Just because the model reports certain results does not mean that they have to be assumed to be credible.

7. Using Seasonality to Your Advantage.

Traffic surveys should be conducted on neutral days and during neutral months of the year. These are ones which are typical in terms of trip-making patterns and traffic conditions. Project schedules mean that this is not always possible, however failure to take proper account of factors such as seasonality can lead to erroneous modelling results.

Figure 4.4 shows the impact of seasonality on roads in Cornwall – a popular tourist destination in the south west of England – and compares traffic patterns there with the UK average.

FIGURE 4.4: EXAMPLE OF SEASONALITY

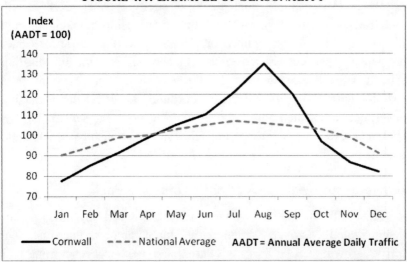

Whereas the national trend demonstrates some seasonality, it is mild in comparison with that recorded in Cornwall. Traffic in Cornwall in August is 35% higher than the annual average. Figure 4.4 shows just how atypical certain months of the year can be. Days of the week can demonstrate similar variability. Compare market-day traffic with that from an average weekday. Without appropriate adjustment, surveys conducted on atypically busy days or during atypically busy months will overstate the amount of trip-making in an area and, *ceteris paribus*, will lead to higher projections of traffic.

8. Remove Inconvenient Truths

This is best illustrated by example. Take a journey time survey involving five separate runs along a toll-free alternative to a proposed toll road. The individual run times are shown in Table 4.2.

TABLE 4.2: JOURNEY TIME SURVEY RESULTS

All Journey Times in Minutes					
Run 1	**Run 2**	**Run 3**	**Run 4**	**Run 5**	**Average**
17	11	14	6	12	12
17	11	14	n/a	12	13.5

The run time average is 12 minutes (top line). However, Run 4 was quicker than the others by some margin. If this is treated as an outlier – and is discarded – the average run time becomes 13.5 minutes (bottom line). This is useful as it degrades the attractiveness of the alternative facility and boosts the competitive standing of the toll road.

The difference between 12 and 13.5 minutes may appear insignificant, however some demand estimation techniques, including the logit formulation described earlier, can be very sensitive to small changes in the characteristics of competing alternatives. Depending on the shape of the curve, these small changes can have a disproportionate impact on the percentage of traffic projected to use the toll road. Traffic advisers using logit models should report how stable their estimates of market capture are to small changes in the competitive landscape – but seldom do.

9. Design & Administer Surveys to Return the Required Results

Transport researchers acknowledge that it is possible to achieve specific results from some survey types through judicious design and administration. Similarly, it is possible to bias the results through poor design and administration. This is particularly true in the case of Stated Preference surveys where respondents' choices between alternative travel options will be influenced by factors such as the range of attribute levels presented to them and the absence of any opt-out choice (forcing an outcome on respondents).

This is not to suggest that Stated Preference techniques are inherently flawed. Good practitioners are alert to the issues mentioned above and should be able to minimise such influences. However credit analysts should look for some comfort in this regard – perhaps ensuring the use of internationally-recognised and experienced firms in this field – alert to the fact that it remains possible to affect survey output through the judicious contexting, selection and definition of the questions being asked to interviewees.

10. The Magic of Expansion/Annualisation Factors

Traffic models focus on critical times of the day such as a weekday AM peak period. Expansion factors are used to gross-up the results, typically to annual estimates (toll revenue per year, for example). The smaller the modelled time period, the more emphasis is placed on these expansion factors – and small changes to the factors can have a significant impact on the final revenue calculations.

Say that a traffic model suggests that, during a weekday AM peak hour, 1,600 vehicles will use a toll road paying an average of $1.50. Two alternative sets of expansion factors are presented in Table 4.3 (as Scenario A and B).

TABLE 4.3: EXPANSION FACTORS AND THEIR INFLUENCE

Expansion Factors	Scenario A	Scenario B
AM Peak Hour as a Fraction of Weekday Daily Traffic	1/8	1/10
Weekday Daily Traffic as a Fraction of Annual Traffic	1/250	1/275
Annual Revenue	**$4.8m**	**$6.6m**

Grossing-up using the expansion factors under Scenario A results in an annual revenue estimate of $4.8m. Using the alternative – yet still plausible – factors under Scenario B, the revenue is $6.6m (nearly 40% higher). This significant difference has nothing to do with the traffic model. It results from the use of different expansion factors.

Traffic advisers should explain their choice of values used and should conduct and report the results from sensitivity tests if revenue projections appear to be particularly factor-dependent. Unlike the simple example given here, the expansion process behind some forecasts can be complex. It is important that analysts understand this process well.

11. Assume that Consumers Act Rationally

It is easy to underestimate the reluctance of some (sometimes many) drivers to paying tolls. Even in circumstances where the time savings appear attractive, it is possible to observe drivers sitting in heavily congested traffic conditions just to avoid paying a relatively modest charge. This may appear to defy logic – and be contrary to what a traffic models suggests – but it can be observed nevertheless. For this reason, credit analysts should pay particular attention to any revealed preference data (from comparable facilities) presented by traffic advisers in support of toll road projections – or, equally, the absence thereof.

12. Assume that Consumers Make the Same Choice Every Time

An urban toll bridge in San Juan, Puerto Rico illustrates this issue well. It caters mainly for commuter traffic heading for the capital's downtown business district. The tariff is $1.50 (cars) and the original traffic model over-estimated demand by 46% in the first full year of operations. Subsequent analysis of travel patterns on the bridge revealed that commuters were not using the bridge in each direction, nor were they using it every day. Commuters were using the bridge selectively. They were more inclined to pay to hurry home than they were to pay to hurry to work – and this effect became more pronounced towards the end of the working week.

The cost proposition in the traffic model was a one-off payment of $1.50 (for x minutes of time saving). However if commuters used the bridge twice a day, five days a week, the cost proposition was $15/week. Although not captured by the model, this was the cost that drivers faced and responded to. Hence their selective use of the asset. Models which fail to capture such behaviour will produce inflated projections of traffic and revenue.

13. Hypothetical Bias: A Helping Hand?

Stated Preference (SP) surveys are widely used in transport studies because they are one of the few techniques that can measure the market and non-market values associated with initiatives such as new toll roads. The technique remains somewhat controversial. The analyst cannot be certain of the accuracy of the SP value estimates since SP surveys are hypothetical in both the payment for and the provision of the service in question. Most of the research suggests that people overestimate the amount they would pay for a service when they do not have to back-up that choice with a real commitment (hard cash). This is called hypothetical bias and is well documented in both laboratory and field settings – see, for example, Murphy et al (2005). Their meta-analysis suggests that mean hypothetical values could be 2.5 to 3 times greater than actual cash payments would be.

There is some limited contradictory research (see Brownstone and Small, 2005) which suggests that SP actually underestimates the amount that people would be willing to pay in real life. Notwithstanding, analysts should be aware that there are professional concerns about SP and hypothetical bias – particularly when interviewees remain uncertain about their responses. The majority view is that, when present, hypothetical bias is likely to overstate (inflate) the consumer response. This is yet another reason why revealed preference data – hard evidence – should be provided alongside SP survey results whenever possible.

14. Grow Your Value of Travel Time Savings

The value of travel time savings (VTTS) is a central concept in toll road demand studies. It is a large topic in itself. Here we will concentrate on just three aspects. The first is the concept of growth in the VTTS, as it is common for traffic consultants to use growth assumptions about the VTTS in toll road forecasting models. The underlying theory suggests that disposable income will grow – in real terms – in the future and hence the value attributed to time savings should also grow in the future. Forecasts of GDP are often used as a proxy for the growth in disposable income, although the actual growth factor applied to VTTS may be higher (eg. 1.2x disposable income growth).

Increasing the value of time savings boosts toll road usage in future years. There may be arguments in support of such an approach – and these should be articulated as required – however the impact of this growth is commonly material, and should be isolated and understood by credit analysts who may feel that, in some situations, it has the scent of equity up-side about it.

There is a second issue regarding time savings that is pertinent to mention here. It concerns small time savings. The conventional approach is to say that the driver who values a time saving of one hour at $20 automatically values a saving of three minutes at $1. This is known as the constant value approach and it has attracted a vocal body of critical opinion. Researchers suggest that small amounts of saved time are inherently less useful than large amounts – particularly if you cannot do anything with the time saved – and that small amounts of saved time may remain unnoticed (and hence unvalued) by travellers. Assumptions about relatively small time savings have a particular relevance in the context of short tolled sections of road, bridges or tunnels. The recent revenue underperformance of some urban toll tunnels in Australia, for example, may, in part, be attributed to overestimating the price consumers are willing to pay to save relatively small amounts of travel time.

Finally there is the issue of VTTS in congested traffic conditions. Some traffic advisers maintain that the VTTS varies according to congestion levels and values over 1.5x the base value have been noted. Traffic advisers draw parallels with the value of waiting time in public transport models (which is typically higher than the value of travel time – reflecting the perception of time passing more slowly while waiting). The impact is for more trips in the model to assign via the tolled facility and the effect – helpfully – compounds in the future as congestion levels deteriorate across the network; encouraging yet more traffic to use the toll road.

15. Overstating the Toll Road Premium

Some traffic models incorporate the use of a 'modal constant' – a toll road premium or bonus – to capture the inherent attractiveness of toll roads. This suggests that if a toll road and its toll-free competitor are matched in generalised cost terms, instead of traffic assigning on a 50:50 basis, proportionately more traffic will use the toll road. The premium is supposed to encapsulate those characteristics of the road not fully estimated in the model (perhaps softer attributes that are more difficult to quantify like ride quality, or perceived safety). The impact of the premium is replicated in models that, alternatively, penalise links that compete with the toll road.

The danger here lies in overestimating the premium – overstating the inherent attractiveness of the asset. This would inflate the revenues. Any toll road premium employed by traffic consultants should be made explicit and should be justified – to the extent of re-running the model in its absence to determine the contribution to revenues made by assumptions about the premium alone.

16. Overstating the Yield

Yield refers to average revenue/vehicle. As most toll roads are dominated by private car use, the yield generally lies close to the tariff paid by private car users. Because of the proportionately higher tariffs, the greater the contribution of trucks and buses to the traffic mix, the higher will be the yield. Overestimating the number of trucks using a toll road will disproportionately inflate aggregate revenues. This is a particular concern as truck usage of toll roads is notoriously challenging to predict and has often been overestimated.

Yield calculations can also be overstated if unrealistic assumptions are made about the take-up of discount programmes offered by the toll road operator. Similarly, unrealistic estimates of toll avoidance and/or exemptions will overstate yield. Analysts need to understand not only what revenues are forecasted, but the composition of these revenues and any (and all) assumptions underpinning them.

17. Reliance on Speculative Development

Future land use plans are a key traffic modelling input – however there may be questions about how committed some development proposals actually are. The reliance that can be placed on land use plans is a challenging issue in transitioning economies or economies experiencing rapid growth – especially under less-regulated planning regimes – however it is also an issue in many developed countries.

Purely speculative developments should be omitted from base case traffic forecasts. Similarly, developments which are expected to result from the building of new toll facilities should be treated cautiously in terms of their contribution to traffic and, hence, toll revenues. Including speculative and generated developments in toll road demand models simply serves to inflate the traffic and revenue projections.

18. The Joy of Induced Demand

It is widely acknowledged that building new highway infrastructure generates traffic. However the relationship is far from clear or consistent. Often toll road traffic forecasters make an assumption about generated (induced) traffic and add this to their forecasts. An upwards adjustment of 10% is not uncommon – however it is seldom rigorously supported.

Analysts should identify if such an adjustment has been made to the traffic figures they are reviewing and then consider the evidence provided in support. In some circumstances the contribution from induced traffic has been removed from base case toll road revenue forecasts reflecting the fact that considerable uncertainty surrounds this revenue contribution. As before, induced traffic helpfully serves to inflate project revenues.

19. Introduce Your Own Toll Discount

There is some evidence to suggest that, in terms of toll road usage, drivers may respond differently to different toll road payment media – particularly non-cash options. By using electronic toll collection (ETC) technologies, drivers do not have to pay the toll at the time/ point of use. Instead, the charge is made to their credit card account and they are billed, in arrears, on a monthly basis. It is suggested that this encourages toll road usage above and beyond what would be expected from a cash-only operation. To capture this effect, traffic modellers talk about a 'perceived ETC discount' – the discount reflecting users' misperceptions of the price paid due to electronic tolling and the payment deferral. Note that this is entirely separate from (and in addition to) any real discount enjoyed by ETC scheme patrons.

In a recent study, the perceived ETC discount was set at 15% and tariffs were reduced to 0.85x their face value. Of course, reducing the price encourages toll road use and inflates the traffic figures. Credit analysts should look for evidence in support of perceived ETC discounts in traffic studies if they are to accept the use of artificially reduced tolls in base case revenue projections.

20. Assume Instant or Quick Ramp-Up

As discussed earlier, ramp-up is the period upon the opening of a new tolled facility when drivers experiment with new routes. It is a period typically characterised by strong growth (from a low base) and it ends when trip-making stabilises into more mature trends. It is notoriously difficult to predict in terms of its depth and duration. Traffic consultants often assume a ramp-up profile based on instinct or weak evidence with questionable transferability.

The use of instant or short ramp-up assumptions runs the danger of inflating early-year revenue forecasts – at a time when financial models may be at their most sensitive. Ramp-up assumptions should be challenged to understand their underpinning rationale. It may be sensible to run sensitivity tests using alternative assumptions to ensure that the financial model remains robust during the early years of project operations and throughout the remaining term of the concession.

21. Ignore Physical (or Operational) Capacity Constraints

It may seem incredible that some forecasts have actually exceeded the physical capacity of their road (in terms of volume/lane/hour) but it has been noted – particularly when these forecasts result, not directly from traffic models, but from traffic model figures extrapolated into the future. Typically no mention is made of widening or the costs (and disruption) involved in capacity expansion. Turning from volume/hour to volume/day, another phenomenon observed has been the fact that some forecasts of daily traffic (AADT) would required roads to operate at peak-hour congestion levels for over 12 (sometimes over 18) hours/day. These highly uncharacteristic flow profiles should certainly raise analytical questions.

The recent development of managed lanes with dynamic pricing – particularly in the US – introduces concerns about how forecasts may exceed a highway's *operational* capacity. On some managed lanes, the tariff is adjusted based on the volume of traffic using the facility. As usage goes up, the toll goes up – with a view to constraining demand such that a certain level of service (or above) can be offered to drivers. Traffic forecasts recently reviewed from one project, however, were so high that they would have degraded the level of service to below that required contractually of the concessionaire. This was not commented upon in the traffic and revenue study report. High-Occupancy Vehicle (HOV) and HOV/toll (HOT) lanes – and other initiatives that fall under the 'managed lane' concept – are relatively new and present particular methodological challenges to traffic modellers. They are commonly crudely or incompletely represented within the model – although this fact is seldom highlighted. Investors and credit analysts reviewing these more innovative tolling applications need to ensure that traffic advisers explain clearly what has been achieved, how and – importantly – the limits of these achievements.

Commentary

The list of 21 ways in which toll road traffic and revenue forecasts can be inflated is not exhaustive. That was not the intention. It is purely indicative. There are others – some of which are highly technical and would require forensic work to uncover (such as the careful positioning of centroid connectors). Other techniques are more general and rely upon clouding detail – such as obscuring daily traffic volumes (which people understand) by reporting vehicle kilometres/year (which no one can). Or obscuring the relationship between traffic and revenue by simply reporting project revenues. This way, the reader has no idea how much traffic is supposed to be paying how much toll. The results cannot be compared or sense-checked with the findings from other studies.

Good traffic consultants know how to fine-tune their models. That is what model calibration is all about. In an environment where prizes are commonly awarded to the bidding team with the highest numbers, fine-tuning may be open to abuse. The purpose of the list is not to alarm investors or credit analysts. It simply demonstrates that it is perfectly possible to inflate the numbers for clients who want inflated numbers, and highlights some key issues to watch out for.

To knowingly inflate traffic and revenue projections is an act of deception – but it is not alone in that regard. Credit analysts reviewing toll road studies should remain alert to two other potential acts of deceit. The first concerns sensitivity tests. Suspicions should arise when sensitivity tests apparently have limited adverse impact on project traffic and/or revenues. This is certainly possible (because of natural hedges or other risk mitigants) but it is not the norm. Good explanations should be provided in support of such results.

The second act of deceit concerns the use of pseudo-science to try to infer a precision of foresight that is simply not be supported by the empirical evidence reviewed earlier. Favoured ploys include the presentation of narrow confidence intervals around base case forecasts and the abuse of exceedance probabilities. Traffic advisers sometimes talk in terms of P95 forecast values – inferring that there is only a 5% probability of that particular number (traffic volume or revenue) not being achieved. However these exceedance probabilities are unlike those associated with scientifically-measurable natural phenomena such as the measurement of wind to determine energy yield predictions for wind farm financings. At best, they result from consultants attempting to re-cast their traffic model in a simple probabilistic framework. At worst, they are simply guesstimates.

Proper analysis of any traffic or toll revenue projections presented as probabilities requires a sound understanding of the probabilistic model construction, the probabilistic variables and their distributions and the correlations among the probabilistic variables. No comfort should ever be taken from P95 figures alone. If there really was as little uncertainty in the forecasts as some sensitivity tests, confidence intervals and P95s have suggested, traffic advisers could remove the legal disclaimers from their reports and could cancel their professional indemnity insurance. These trends have not been observed to date.

TEST YOURSELF...

Having reviewed a toll road traffic and revenue forecasting report you should be able to answer 'yes' to the following five questions:

1. Do I understand tolling in the host country? (history, existing applications, political support, public acceptability).

2. Do I understand the road? (where it is, its purpose, its features, its price, its competitive context – today and in the future).

3.   Do I understand the data? (data sources, surveys, limitations).

4.   Do I understand the market? (who will use the road, why, composition of users, income levels, sensitivity to price, current driving conditions).

5.   Do I understand growth? (underlying assumptions, key drivers, ramp-up, how growth rates have been applied).

CONCLUDING REMARKS

The network equilibrium models used today as the basis for making traffic forecasts were developed 50 years ago to help in the design of post-war freeway systems and for the evaluation of urban or regional transportation plans at a strategic level. With some tweaks, these models are now being applied in ways, for purposes and with a required level of precision simply not originally anticipated. They have been used for air quality conformity calculations, for example, but have been found to be deficient in that regard. The empirical evidence presented earlier suggests that the same conclusion holds for their use in the preparation of detailed toll revenue projections. However they represent the state-of-the-practice for the traffic consultant and, when used intelligently and within their limitations, provide useful insights into possible future travel behaviour and network usage. That is the good news.

The bad news is that the future looks to be even more challenging for the toll road traffic model and modeller. Initiatives such as HOT lanes and managed lanes – with dynamic pricing – will require even more sophisticated and granular modelling capabilities. Combine this with the fact that toll roads, globally, continue to be one of the most popular asset classes to be offered to the private sector as concessions and you will understand why investors – and analysts acting on their behalf – might want to look inside the black-box of a traffic model. Hence this guide.

In the world of credit, however, toll road traffic and revenue reports are not stand-alone documents. Our understanding of the traffic story needs to be set in the wider context of the overall transaction package. At the outset it was noted that modelling error tolerance is generally low in the financial services sector. All of the evidence suggests that this should not be so. Lenders require flexibility within a transaction package to allow for the inevitable departures from forecasting expectations. This flexibility will generally find expression in the financial features of a transaction structure such as reasonable and manageable debt burdens, adequate reserve accounts, contingency funds, coverage ratios, gearing with sufficient equity participation and a project 'tail' (generating additional project revenues after the scheduled maturity of the loan). However bankable projects need to be based on sound and supported commercial propositions. Project liquidity (and liquidity support) is essential, but liquidity alone does not make bad projects good – and structure is a poor substitute for substance.

This guide set out to arm analysts with practical information that could be used to help to interpret toll road traffic and revenue projections. When dealing with the future it is not possible to eliminate uncertainty. With information and understanding, however – combined with a level-head – we might just be able to live with it a little more comfortably.

GLOSSARY

A

Alignment
The horizontal and vertical ground plan of a road or other facility.

Annualisation Factors
Factors used to expand the data from the modelled time periods to represent a full year.

Annual Average Daily Traffic (AADT)
Total traffic for the year divided by 365.

B

Base-Year Model
A baseline against which forecasting can be undertaken. The base-year model provides a representation of the transport system and travel patterns as they exist today.

C

Calibration
The process of comparing the parameters of a traffic model with real-world observations or measurements and making subsequent adjustments to ensure that the model realistically represents today's traffic environment. Calibration typically compares modelled traffic flows with traffic counts on specific links or modelled journey times/speeds with survey observations.

Capacity
The maximum sustainable flow (vehicles/hour) past a defined

point or over a section of road during a defined time period, under prevailing traffic and roadway conditions.

Capture Rate

The proportion of **In-Scope Trips** that elect to use a toll road.

Car Pool

An arrangement where people share the use and cost of a private car when travelling to and from pre-arranged destinations.

Centroid

An assumed point in a zone that represents the origin or destination of all trips to/from that zone.

Centroid Connector

Centroid connectors link the centroids of zones to the highway network. All of the minor streets which connect the houses, offices and/or factories in a zone to the modelled road network are 'collapsed' into one or two centroid connectors.

Collector/Distributor

A road located between, and running parallel to, the main lanes of a highway and its frontage roads or local streets. Controls access and smoothes the traffic movements between the main lanes and the frontage roads. Also reduces weaving – and increases capacity – on the main highway itself.

Cordon

An imaginary boundary drawn across an area. The volumes on the links crossing the cordon are typically summed to understand the amount of trips entering and exiting an area.

D

Design Speed

The maximum safe speed that can be maintained over a specified section of highway. Dictates which geometric design standards are used. Differs from posted speed (the legal speed limit)

Desire Line

A graphical representation of the demand for travel between two points, drawn as a straight line from an origin to a destination (the line width being scaled to reflect the strength of the demand).

Deterrence

As in a 'deterrence function'. A measure of the disincentive to travel due to spatial separation. May be a composite of distance and travel time. Known also as impedance.

Disutility of Travel

A measure of dissatisfaction as perceived by a consumer which is used in traffic models (and economics) as the cost of making a trip.

E

Elasticity (of Demand)

A measure of the sensitivity of demand for a toll road (or commodity) to a change in price. It equals the percentage change in the demand for a toll road that results from a one percent change in price. The greater the elasticity, the more price sensitive is the demand.

Electronic Toll Collection (ETC)

Electronic systems that collect tolls without requiring vehicles with a transponder – an electronic 'tag' – to stop. Involves two-way radio communications between moving vehicles and gantry-mounted or roadside sensors. Usually comprised of three sub-systems: one to identify the vehicle, one to classify the vehicle and one to detect violators for enforcement purposes.

Equilibrium Assignment

A traffic assignment algorithm that takes into account the build-up of traffic and the ensuing changes in travel times when allocating trips to links. The algorithm solves for an equilibrium solution for network flows (ie. overall demand and system performance are balanced in the model).

External Trip
A trip with either its origin or destination lying outside the study area.

F

Floating Car
A data collection method relying on a surveyor's car driving in a traffic stream at the prevailing speed – primarily used to collect journey time/speed data.

Free Flow Speed
The uninterrupted speed of traffic when there are no or few other vehicles present (traffic density is almost zero).

Functional Classification
The grouping of highways and streets into classes according to the character of the service they are intended to provide.

Furness
A matrix modification method used to extrapolate trip distribution on the basis of zonal growth factors and iterative proportional fitting. Known also as the 'Fratar method'.

G

GEH Score
Used in model calibration, this goodness-of-fit statistic measures the difference between modelled traffic flows and actual traffic counts, taking specific account of the absolute magnitude of the counts. The better the match, the closer the GEH Score is to zero.

Generalised Cost
The composite cost of travel which includes monetary expenses and the 'cost' of travel time (ie. travel time expressed as a monetary cost). A key determinant of trip distribution and assignment in traffic models.

Generated Traffic
The additional travel resulting from a transport improvement

(eg. build of a new road) which would not have otherwise occurred. Known also as 'induced traffic'.

Grade Separation

The vertical separation between intersecting roads, one traffic stream travelling over the other – so that crossing movements (which would otherwise conflict) are at different levels.

Gravity Model

A model of the interaction (eg. travel) between two population centres based on Newton's Law. Two bodies in the universe attract each other in proportion to the product of their masses and inversely as the squared distance between them.

H

High Occupancy/Toll (HOT) Lanes

A derivative of HOV lanes (see below). Reserved traffic lanes which low occupancy vehicles can use for a toll whereas high occupancy vehicles travel for free (or at a discount).

High Occupancy Vehicle (HOV) Lanes

Reserved traffic lanes for the exclusive use of vehicles with a defined minimum number of occupants (>1) such as shared cars, vanpools, minibuses and buses. Typically denoted as HOV2+ or HOV3+.

Highway Capacity Manual

[USA] Standard guidelines and procedures for roadway and intersection capacity design and analysis.

Highway Capacity Software (HCS)

The software implementation of the Highway Capacity Manual.

I

Indifference Curve

A graph of the relative demand for two competing routes (perhaps one, a toll road) for which the utility derived is the same and therefore drivers have no choice preference.

Induced Traffic
   See **Generated Traffic**.

In-Scope Traffic
   The market for a toll road. Traffic movements in a study area which might (given the right circumstances) use the toll road. Compare with **Market Capture**: traffic movements which *would* use the toll road.

Internal Trips
   A trip with both its origin and destination in the study area.

Iteration
   Trip assignment aims to ensure that every trip in the traffic model takes the lowest generalised cost route between its origin and destination. To do this, the model tests numerous routeing combinations. Each of these tests is an iteration of the model. Successive iterations lead to the point where the model achieves equilibrium ('converges').

J

Journey Purpose
   The reason a person chooses to make a trip. In traffic models, journey purposes are commonly divided into categories such as:-

* **Home-Based Work**: travelling from home to work (and back again);
* **Home-Based Other**: travelling from home to a non-work location (eg. for shopping or leisure);
* **Home-Based Employer's Business**: travelling from home to a destination when you are on your employer's time as soon as you leave the house;
* **Non-Home-Based Employer's Business**: travel during your employer's time (such as attending a business meeting);
* **Non-Home-Based Other**: travelling from a non-home-based origin to a destination (such as work to shops during lunchtime).

K

K-Factor

A factor that reflects the proportion of daily traffic occurring (or expected to occur) in the peak hour.

L

Level of Service (LOS)

A qualitative measure (from 'A' to 'F') of operating conditions on a road and drivers' perceptions of these conditions. LOS reflects speed, travel time, freedom to manoeuvre, traffic interruptions, comfort and convenience. LOS A represents free-flow conditions. LOS F is forced flow operations at low speed with many stoppages.

Link

In a traffic model, a link represents a section of roadway and its characteristics such as length, number of lanes, capacity, free-flow speed and speed/flow relationship (see below). Links are defined by a starting and ending node (see later).

Logit Model

A choice model that assumes an individual maximises utility in choosing between available alternatives. In a traffic model, the logit function calculates the propensity to use a toll road as a function of the relative cost or travel time between the tolled and the non-tolled route.

Loop Detector

An in-road detector (inductive wire loop) that senses the passage or presence of a vehicle near the sensor.

M

Managed Lanes

Designated traffic lanes that use a variety of traffic management strategies such a pricing (eg. real time variable tolling), metering or access control to most efficiently use existing capacity.

Matrix

A matrix (trip matrix or trip table) is a tabular representation showing the number of trips between every origin zone and destination zone in a traffic model.

Matrix Estimation

Trip matrices provide a framework for representing every origin-destination movement in a study area (eg. in Madrid). However it is clearly not possible to obtain information about everybody in Madrid and all of their trip-making. Survey data are collected from a representative sample of travellers and the data are expanded to represent the entire matrix. Thus the total matrix is estimated based on the survey data.

ME2

Maximum entropy matrix estimation. An efficient and particularly cost-effective technique for estimating or updating trip matrices based on observed traffic counts.

Microsimulation

The modelling of individual vehicle movements for the purpose of assessing the traffic performance – at a detailed level – of roads or intersections

Mode

A particular form of travel/transport: cars, light goods vehicles (LGVs), heavy goods vehicles (HGVs), buses and trains (including subways and trams). Walking and cycling are modes of transport too, but remain largely irrelevant in the context of toll road studies. Intermodal refers to the connections between modes. Multimodal refers to the availability of alternative transport options.

Mode Choice

When assigning trips to a network, a traffic model has to allocate these trips to the different modes of transport available to travellers – this is mode choice. Mode choice is determined principally by generalised cost (travellers taking the lowest 'cost' option available to them) and household car availability. If there is no modal competition to a toll road (either today or in the future), mode choice can be ignored and a highway-only model can substitute for one that offers multi-modal modelling capabilities.

Monte Carlo Simulation

In the right circumstances, Monte Carlo simulation can be useful for modelling phenomena with significant uncertainty in inputs. Instead of using point estimates for the input variables, they are defined in terms of probability distributions. The output variable (eg. flow on a tolled link in a given period) will similarly be presented as a probability distribution rather than a single number.

Neutral Day/Month

When talking about surveys, a neutral day is one that is typical in terms of trip-making patterns and traffic conditions (close to the average). Sunday is not a neutral day. Similarly, August and December are, in most countries, not neutral months. Surveys conducted outside of neutral days/months will be unrepresentative and this will impact on model accuracy.

N

Network

The highway network as it is reflected in the traffic model – represented through a series of links and nodes.

Node

A node is a connection between highway sections in the traffic model (links) and is often – though not always – some form of intersection/junction where delays occur due to the interaction of traffic moving from one link to another.

P

Passenger Car Unit (PCU)

A measure involving the conversion of different vehicle types into equivalent passenger cars in terms of operating characteristics. A truck would have a PCU rating of 2.5, meaning that it typically takes up 2.5 times the road space of an average passenger car.

Peak Hour Factor

The hourly volume (during the maximum-volume hour of the day) divided by the peak 15 minute flow rate. A measure of traffic demand fluctuation within the peak hour itself.

Peak Spreading

The lengthening of the peak period caused by the earlier (and later) departure times of travellers trying to avoid increased peak period congestion by travelling in the 'shoulders' of the peak.

Platoon

Vehicles travelling together as a group (or convoy) along a link, because of signal controls or highway geometrics.

Probability Model

See **Monte Carlo Simulation**.

R

Ramp-Up

Ramp-up is the period upon the opening of a toll road characterised by strong growth in usage – from a low base – as travellers become accustomed to the new facility and its features.

Revealed Preference (RP)

An individual's preference that is identified through observation of an actual choice and the attributes associated with that choice. Compare with **Stated Preference**.

Roadside Interview (RSI) Survey

A roadside interview survey involves stopping a sample of drivers (or surveying them when they are stationary) and asking questions primarily about the location of the origin and destination of their current trip. This information is subsequently attributed (coded) to zones.

S

Screenline

An imaginary line drawn across a number of (typically parallel) roads entering one area to build-up a picture of combined travel movements along a corridor, as opposed to those on individual roads.

Select Link Analysis

Select Link Analysis allows you understand, in some detail, trip-making patterns on a single link in the traffic model's network. Conducting this analysis on a modelled toll road (the selected link) creates a trip matrix which describes the origins and destinations of travellers using that particular road alone.

Shadow Toll

Reimbursement payments made by governments (as opposed to road users) to private sector operators of toll roads based, at least in part, on the number of vehicles using the road.

Single Occupant Vehicle (SOV)

A privately-operated vehicle whose only occupant is the driver.

Speed/Flow Relationship

Describes how traffic speed varies along a link with flow. Enables journey times to be calculated for a given volume of vehicular flow. Of most use outside urban areas (within urban areas journey times are more influenced by intersections and intersection capacity).

Stated Preference (SP)

Stated Preference methods are widely used in travel behaviour research to identify likely consumer responses to choice situations which are not revealed in the market. SP techniques base demand estimates on an analysis of the response to hypothetical (yet realistic) choices.

Strategic Traffic Model

A strategic traffic model (as opposed to a detailed one) focuses on the key movements taking place across a study area using main roads. The model does not attempt to represent minor roads in the network.

T

Traffic Analysis Zone (TAZ)

[USA] A Traffic Analysis Zone is a special area for tabulating traffic-related data, particularly journey-to-work and place-of-work statistics. Usually consists of one or more census blocks, block groups or census tracts.

Trip Assignment

Trip assignment involves loading all journeys (from the trip matrix) onto the network. During assignment, the model iterates to find the cheapest generalised cost paths (routes) for trip-makers through the network.

Trip Distribution

Trip Distribution – the second step in the traditional four-stage model – matches up the trip ends (the demand for travel to/from each zone) calculated at the Trip Generation stage. The trips generated by each zone are distributed to a set of destination zones. The model determines, for every journey from each zone, to which zone that journey will travel.

Trip End

Each trip in the model has two trip ends; an origin zone and a destination zone. In a demand matrix, a set of origin trip ends (productions) is obtained by summing the row totals to give the number of trips coming out of each zone. The column totals represent the number of trips going into each zone (attractions).

Trip Generation

Trip Generation is the process by which the number of trips produced by and – separately – attracted to each zone in the model is calculated. The production end (trip origin) typically reflects household composition, income, or car ownership in a particular zone. The attraction end (trip destination) typically reflects employment levels in that zone.

Trip Table

See **Matrix**.

U

Utility

The value to a decision-maker of a particular choice alternative. A rational decision-maker is assumed to maximise utility when making a choice (eg. selecting a particular route for their trip).

V

Validation

Validation is the process of independently checking the accuracy/robustness of model calibration. It should be conducted using data held-back from the calibration process itself. Validation determines whether a traffic model is fit for purpose by comparing the model's predictions with observations or measurements.

Value of Travel Time Savings (VTTS)

The monetary value attached to the possibility to save a determined amount of travel time. The most important benefit category aimed at justifying investments in transport infrastructure by public administrations and a key concept in toll road traffic demand studies.

Vehicle Miles of Travel (VMT)

A measure of total travel calculated by multiplying the total number of vehicles by the respective distance by which each has travelled.

Volume to Capacity (V/C) Ratio

The ratio of vehicle flow on a road to the capacity of that road. The V/C ratio is a measure of congestion (or, alternatively, the sufficiency of highway capacity). May be used to define problem areas (hot spots) on a highway network. Ratios of less than 0.5 indicate free-flow traffic conditions. Between 0.5 and 0.8 suggests slow-down conditions. Above 0.8 is start-stop conditions and beyond 1.0 signifies flow breakdown.

W

Weaving Area/Segment

A section of roadway where two or more vehicle streams have to cross each other's paths through lane-changing manoeuvres (without the aid of traffic signals).

Willingness to Pay

The amount an individual is willing to pay to acquire a good or service (eg. use a toll road). The good or service may be one that is bought and sold (a market good) or not (a non-market good). Willingness to pay varies with income level.

Z

Zone

The study area of a traffic model is divided into separate zones, based largely upon homogenous land use. Smaller zones tend to be used in busy urban areas and nearest to the focus for the model (the toll road). Larger zones will be used in rural areas and in places far from the model's focus. In a traffic model for a toll road in Scotland, for example, England may be represented as one or two very large zones. No greater detail than that is required. Large or unusual generators of travel demand (such as shopping malls or airports) may be allocated their own zone. Zone boundaries tend to follow natural features such as rivers and/or be consistent with administrative (eg. census) areas. Zones are where trips begin and end.

BIBLIOGRAPHY

Bain R and Wilkins M (2002), *The Evolution of DBFO Payment Mechanisms: One More for the Road*, Standard & Poor's, London.

Bain R and Wilkins M (2002), *The Credit Implications of Traffic Risk in Start-Up Toll Facilities*, Standard & Poor's, London.

Bain R and Plantagie J W (2003), *Traffic Forecasting Risk: Study Update 2003*, Standard & Poor's, London.

Bain R and Plantagie J W (2004), *Traffic Forecasting Risk: Study Update 2004*, Standard & Poor's, London.

Bain R and Polakovic L (2005), *Traffic Forecasting Risk Study 2005: Through Ramp-Up and Beyond*, Standard & Poor's, London.

Barton-Aschman Associates Inc. and Cambridge Systematics Inc. (1997), *Model Validation and Reasonableness Checking Manual*, prepared for the Travel Model Improvement Program, Federal Highways Administration.

Beimborn E, Kennedy R and Schaefer W (1996), *Inside the Blackbox: Making Transportation Models Work for Livable Communities*, Citizens for a Better Environment.

Boyce D (2004), *Forecasting Travel on Congested Urban Transportation Networks: Review and Prospects for Network Equilibrium Models*, TRISTAN V: The Fifth Triennial Symposium on Transportation Analysis, Le Gosier, Guadeloupe, June 13-14 2004.

Brinkman P A (2003), *The Ethical Challenges and Professional Responses of Travel Demand Forecasters*, PhD dissertation, University of California, Berkeley.

Brownstone D and Small K (2005), *Valuing Time and Reliability: Assessing the Evidence from Road Pricing Demonstrations*, Transportation Research Part A – Policy and Practice, 39(4), pp.279-293.

Department of Transport (1995), *8th Scheme Forecast Monitoring Report*, Department of Transport, UK.

Fitch Ratings (1999), *Challenges of Start-Up Toll Roads*, Project Finance Special Report.

Fitch Ratings (2007), *Global Toll Road Rating Guidelines*, Criteria Report.

Flyvbjerg B, Bruzelius N and Rothengatter W (2005), *How (In)accurate are Demand Forecasts in Public Works Projects?*, Journal of American Planning Association, Volume 71, No. 2, Spring 2005, American Planning Association, Chicago, IL.

Giglio, J (1998), *Why Governments Lie – Why Governments ALWAYS Lie About the Cost of Public Work Projects – and Why People Want Them To*, The American Outlook – Ideas for the Future, Vol. 1.

Hensher D and Goodwin P (2003), *Using Values of Travel Time Savings for Toll Roads: Avoiding Some Common Errors*, Transport Policy, 11(2), pp. 171-181, ISSN 0967070X.

Lemp J and Kockelman K (2008), *Understanding and Accommodating Risk and Uncertainty in Toll Road Projects*, submitted for presentation at the 88th Annual Meeting of the Transportation Research Board, 11-15th January 2009, Washington DC.

Li Z and Hensher D (2009), *Toll Roads in Australia*, Institute of Transport and Logistics Studies, University of Sydney, March.

Mackett R (1998), *Why Are Travel Demand Forecasts So Often Wrong (and Does it Matter)?*, UTSG Annual Conference, January 1998, Dublin.

Mierzejewski E (1997), *Recognizing Uncertainty in the Transportation Planning Process: A Strategic Planning Approach*, TRB 76th Annual Meeting, January 12-16 1997, Washington DC.

Moody's Investor Service (2000), *Rating Methodology: Start-Up Toll Roads*.

Moody's Investor Service (2006), *Rating Methodology: Operational Toll Roads*.

Morgan J P (1997), *Examining Toll Road Feasibility Studies*, Municipal Finance Journal, Volume 18, No. 1, Spring 1997.

Muller R and Buono K (2002), *Start-Up Toll Roads: Separating Winners from Losers*, Municipal Credit Monitor, J P Morgan, New York NY.

Murphy J, Allen P, Stevens T and Weatherhead D (2005), *A Meta-Analysis of Hypothetical Bias in Contingent Valuation*, Environmental and Resource Economics, 30(3): pp.313-325.

Ortúzar J de D and Willumsen L G (2001), *Modelling Transport*, Third Edition, Wiley, Chichester.

Pavithra P and Levinson D (2008), *Post-Construction Evaluation of Traffic Forecast Accuracy*, Department of Civil Engineering, University of Minnesota, Minneapolis MN.

Standing Advisory Committee on Trunk Road Assessment (1994), *Trunk Roads and the Generation of Traffic*, HMSO, London.

State of Florida Department of Transportation (2002), *Project Traffic Forecasting Handbook*.

Transportation Research Board (2006), *Estimating Toll Road Demand and Revenue: A Synthesis of Highway Practice*, NCHRP Synthesis 364, Transportation Research Board, Washington DC.

Transportation Research Board (2007), *Metropolitan Travel Forecasting: Current Practice and Future Direction*, Special Report 288, Transportation Research Board, Washington DC.

URS (2006), *The Long-Term Projection of Traffic and Revenues for Equity Analysis Purposes*, Toll Studies Group, URS Corporation.

Vassallo J M (2007), *Why Traffic Forecasts in PPP Contracts are Often Overestimated?*, EIB University Research Sponsorship Programme, EIB, Luxembourg.

Washington State Transportation Commission (2006), *Limitations of Studies to Advance Toll Projects*, Washington State Comprehensive Tolling Study, Final Report, Volume 2, Background Paper 6.

Zhao Y and Kockelman K M (2002), *The Propagation of Uncertainty Through Travel Demand Models: An Exploratory Analysis*, Annals of Regional Science 36(1).

APPENDIX A

STANDARD & POOR'S TRAFFIC RISK INDEX

Project Attributes	Traffic Risk Index									
	1	2	3	4	5	6	7	8	9	10
Tolling Regime	Shadow tolls					User-paid tolls				
Tolling Culture	Toll roads well established					No toll roads in the country				
Tariff Escalation	Generous escalation formula, no government approval					All tariff hikes require government approval				
Forecast Horizon	Near-term forecasts required					Long-term (30+ year) forecasts required				
Infrastructure Details	Facility already open					Facility at the very earliest stages of planning				
	Estuarial crossings					Dense, urban networks				
	Extension of existing road					Green field site				
	Alignment: strong rationale (inc. tolling points & intersections)					Confused/unclear road objectives (not where people want to go)				
	Alignment: strong economics					Alignment: strong politics!				
	Clear understanding of future-highway network					Many options for network extensions exist				
	Highly congested corridor					Limited/no congestion				
	Few competing roads					Many alternative routes				
	Clear competitive advantage					Weak competitive advantage				
	Only highway competition					Multi-modal competition				
	Stand-alone facility					Reliance on other, proposed highway improvements				
	Good, high-capacity connectors					Hurry-up-and-wait!				
	'Active' competition protection (eg. traffic calming, truck bans)					Autonomous authorities can do what they want (and do!)				
Surveys/Data Collection	Easy-to-collect (laws exist)					Difficult/dangerous to collect				
	Up-to-date					Historical information				
	Locally-calibrated parameters					Parameters imported from elsewhere (another country?)				

	Existing zone framework (widely used)	Develop zone framework from scratch
	Experienced surveyors	No culture of data collection
Users: Private	Clear market segment(s)	Unclear market segments
	Few, key origins & destinations	Multiple origins & destinations
	Dominated by single journey purpose (eg. commute, airport)	Multiple journey purposes
	High income, time sensitive market	Average/low income market
	Tolls in line with existing facilities	Tolls far higher than the norm
	Simple toll structure	Complex toll structure (local discounts, frequent users)
	Flat demand profile (time-of-day, day-of-week etc.)	Highly seasonal and/or 'peaky' demand profile
Users: Commercial	Fleet operator pays toll	Owner-driver pays toll
	Clear time and operating cost savings	Unclear competitive advantage
	Simple route choice decision-making	Complicated route choice decision-making
	Strong compliance with weight restrictions	Overloading of trucks is commonplace
Macro-environment	Strong, stable economy	Weak/transitioning economy
	Strict land-use planning regime	Weak planning controls/enforcement
	Stable, predictable population growth	Population forecast dependent on many, exogenous factors
Traffic Growth	Driven by/correlated with existing, established and predictable factors	Reliance upon future factors, new developments, structural changes etc.
	High car ownership	Low/growing car ownership

APPENDIX B

THE TRAFFIC RISK INDEX: WORKED EXAMPLE I

In this worked example, horizontal bars are used to represent the level of investor exposure against each of the individual risk categories.

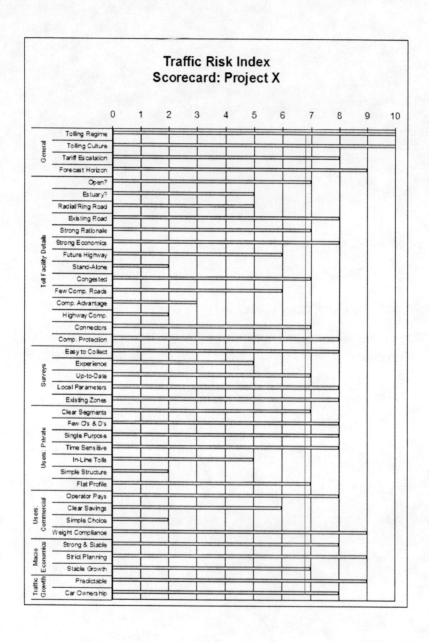

Traffic Risk Index
Scorecard: Project X

APPENDIX C

THE TRAFFIC RISK INDEX: WORKED EXAMPLE II

In this worked example traffic consultants have extended the Traffic Risk Index to include, alongside their risk scores, comments reflecting their justification for these scores.

Project Attributes	Traffic Risk Index										Toll Road	
	1	2	3	4	5	6	7	8	9	10	Risk Score	Comments
Tolling Regime	Shadow tolls				User-paid tolls						8	Sensitive to willingness to pay.
Tolling Culture	Toll roads well established – data on actual use is available				No toll roads in the country – uncertainty over toll acceptance						7	Tolling is currently limited to two existing sections of motorway.
Tariff Escalation	Flexible rate setting/escalation formula, no government approval				All tariff hikes require regulatory approval						6	Government has powers to lower tolls.
Forecast horizon	Near-term forecasts required				Long-term (30+ year) forecasts required						7	Forecasts required over 30+ years from opening year.
Toll-facility details	Facility already open				Facility at the very earliest stages of planning						5	Sections of toll road already open but currently toll free.
	Estuarial crossings				Dense, urban networks						5	This is an interurban highway.
	Radial corridors into urban areas				Ring-roads/beltways around urban areas						4	Connects radial routes into cities.
	Extension of existing road				Green-field site						4	Part upgrade of existing corridor/part greenfield.
	Alignment: strong rationale (inc. tolling points & intersections)				Confused/unclear road objectives (not where people want to go)						2	Long established alignment with proven traffic patterns.

Traffic Risk Index			Toll Road
Alignment: strong economics	Alignment: strong politics	5	Long established north-south corridor.
Clear understanding of future-highway network	Many options for network extensions exist	3	Information on road programme provided by Govt.
Stand-alone (single) facility	Reliance on other, proposed highway improvements	3	Feeder roads are recognised funding priorities.
Highly congested corridor	Limited/no congestion	5	Localised congestion on city approaches and at intersections.
Few competing roads	Many alternative routes	4	Competition of alternative routes hindered by limited capacity and urban congestion.
Clear competitive advantage	Weak competitive advantage	3	Significant time savings.
Only highway competition	Multimodal competition	2	Negligible competition from rail.
Good, high-capacity connectors	Hurry-up-and-wait	2	Connects with other interurban highways, bypasses urban areas.

	Traffic Risk Index			Toll Road
Surveys/data collection	'Active' competition protection (e.g. traffic calming, truck bans)	Autonomous authorities can do what they want	4	Truck ban in urban centres along corridor. Speed enforcement cameras in use.
	Easy-to-collect (laws exist)	Difficult/dangerous to collect	3	Bad weather is main risk to data collection
	Experienced surveyors	No culture of data collection	2	Used experienced survey specialists.

APPENDIX D

SUGGESTED TABLE OF CONTENTS FOR A LENDERS' TRAFFIC & REVENUE STUDY REPORT

TABLE OF CONTENTS *[indicative page count in brackets]*

Executive Summary [*5*]

1. **Introduction** [*5*]
   - Summary description of the scheme/project. Concept. Supporting maps – keep it simple. What, exactly, is the 'product' being offered to drivers?
   - Background/planning rationale. Promoter's objectives. Short history. Extent of scheme support and/or controversy. Tolling plan/strategy.

2. **Market Overview** [*10*]
   - Define/describe study/catchment area. Predominant land use(s). Demographics.
   - Supply-side characteristics. Competitive context of the facility – today/tomorrow, multimodal competition? Supply-side risks.
   - Demand-side characteristics (overview). Historical trends. Key flows/volumes. Traffic conditions.   Key origin-destination movements. Spatial distribution. Temporal distribution. Seasonality. Journey purpose. Traffic mix.

3. **Study Methodology** [*5*] **(append technical details as necessary)**
   - Non-technical overview (flow-diagram?). Approach taken to modelling. Why? Software used. Why?
   - Zoning system – description and rationale for definition/use. Strengths/weaknesses.
   - What modelling periods? Why? How to take account of non-modelled periods?
   - Expansion/annualisation factors.
   - Constraints and/or risks associated with the study methodology.

4. **Survey Data (and/or input data)** [*5*]
   - Survey programme definition. Why? Limitations. Results.
   - Other sources of data. Integrity? Results.
   - Traffic assignment/toll choice model. Critique.

5. **Base Year Model Calibration/Validation** [*5*]
- Input assumptions. Method(s) of calibration/validation. Why? Link volumes/screenline volumes. Supporting maps. Travel times/speeds. Origin-destination calibration? Use of matrix estimation (how)?
- Calibration/validation results.
- Weaknesses/limitations and implications.

6. **Traffic & Revenue Forecasts** [*10*]
- Modelled years versus interpolation/extrapolation. Network changes.
- Growth assumptions. Sources. How has growth been incorporated? At what level? Why? Socio-economic projections. Land use projections.
- Summary table of all modelling assumptions (providing justification).
- Clear explanation of the link between traffic and revenue forecasts (real/nominal figures?).
- Presentation of results.

7. **Sensitivity Testing/Scenario Analysis** [*10*]
- Frank description of model uncertainties – which variables, and by how much?
- Sensitivity tests/scenario analysis and results.
- Monte Carlo simulation (if used) – variables, distributions, justification, correlations and critique.
- Conclusions.

Appendices
- Append any and all supporting material (especially technical documentation).

ABOUT THE AUTHOR

Robert Bain is a Chartered Civil Engineer. He was a traffic and revenue consultant for 15 years, conducting international toll road feasibility studies for private sector investors and public sector promoters. More recently he moved into financial services and was employed as a credit analyst with Standard & Poor's, working in the agency's Infrastructure Finance Ratings practice for five years. As a Director in the London-based transportation team he was responsible for credits in the road, rail, airport and bus sectors. Robert's portfolio covered corporate issuers and structured finance transactions – typically project finance deals and securitisations.

Robert holds a PhD from the Institute for Transport Studies at the University of Leeds. He is a Fellow of the Institution of Highways and Transportation and a Fellow of the Institution of Civil Engineers. He is currently retained by Standard & Poor's on a freelance basis and runs his own specialist consultancy providing technical support services to institutional investors, insurance companies and infrastructure funds.

Printed in the United States
145717LV00002B/3/P

9 780956 152718